THE CHANGING FACE OF
HAMMERSMITH AND FULHAM

Hammersmith & Fulham
Serving our Community

THE CHANGING FACE OF
HAMMERSMITH AND FULHAM

Jane Kimber and Francis Serjeant

breedon **books**
PUBLISHING

First published in Great Britain in 2002 by
The Breedon Books Publishing Company Limited
Breedon House, 3 The Parker Centre,
Derby, DE21 4SZ.

ISBN 1 85983 295 4

Printed and bound by Butler & Tanner, Frome, Somerset, England.
Cover printing by Lawrence-Allen Colour Printers, Weston-super-Mare,
Somerset.

Contents

Acknowledgements

All the pictures in this book have been selected from the collection of photographs held by Hammersmith and Fulham Archives and Local History Centre. Thanks are due to the following for granting permission to reproduce certain photographs in the book: Mrs E. Fincham, London Metropolitan Archives, London's Transport Museum, Marks & Spencer Company Archive, The Public Record Office and Mr G. Wombwell. The authors apologise for any omissions from the list caused by failure to trace copyright holders. The authors would also like to thank the photographer John Rogers, who was commissioned to take a number of contemporary photographs for the book. Mrs Christine Bayliss, formerly Local History Librarian of Hammersmith and Fulham, took several of the photographs reproduced, especially of the late 1980s–90s redevelopment of the Hammersmith Broadway site. Mr R.E. Rodrigues provided information for the caption to the photograph of Fulham Gas Works. Finally the authors would like to thank their colleague Mrs Anne Wheeldon for her assistance with research during the preparation of the book.

Introduction

The visual collections of Hammersmith and Fulham Archives and Local History Centre form a unique record of the changing appearance of the borough. They consist of some 60,000 photographs, about 600 paintings and a smaller number of old prints, engravings and postcards. Images of Hammersmith and Fulham can also be found elsewhere, in private collections or in repositories such as the Guildhall Library and Art Gallery, London Metropolitan Archives, the National Monuments Record and London's Transport Museum. The Centre's holdings, however, form the premier collection relating to the borough.

Before photography was invented in about 1840, paintings and old prints provided the only visual record of a few of the most important streets and buildings of the area. The Centre has relatively few photographs dating from the middle decades of the 19th century, and it is not until the 1890s that the collection begins to be significant. The golden age of photography lasted from between about 1900 and 1914, partly because there was a fashion throughout the country for publishing local views as postcards. The majority of the Centre's collection was donated, but in the 1970s and 80s Mrs Christine Bayliss, then Local History Librarian of Fulham, was active in recording change in the borough, for example photographing buildings that were soon to be pulled down. The Centre is constantly adding to its stock, and some of the photographs in this book were taken in 2001 by John Rogers, former Borough Photographer of the Royal Borough of Kensington and Chelsea.

Our perception of what the borough looked like before the age of photography must be formed from the few surviving artists' impressions, from maps and from the descriptions found in documents and books. By the 17th century Fulham Town was a large village, clustered around the High Street and the parish church, close to Fulham Palace. The old wooden Fulham Bridge was built in 1729, and about 20 years later a Swedish traveller described Fulham as 'a pretty town with several smooth streets. All the houses are of brick, very beautifully built, some of which belong(ing) to gentlemen... in London are handsomely built... the country here is everywhere nothing but a garden and a pleasaunce.' The principal roads leading to Fulham were in bad repair, and one of the reasons for building St Paul's Church as a chapel-of-ease in Hammersmith in 1631 was because it was so difficult to get down to the river for services at All Saints. West of Fulham Palace, malthouses, limekilns and a chalk wharf had been established by the late 18th century at Crabtree, where there was also an inn and a ferry. Further up the river lay the important estate of Brandenburgh House, built in the reign of Charles I by the slave-trader Sir Nicholas Crisp, occupied briefly by the unlucky Queen Caroline (wife of George IV) and pulled down in 1822.

The hamlet of Sands End had only 35 ratepayers in 1739 and, until the end of the 19th century, it consisted of a few private houses and some market gardens and orchards. The site of Townmead Road had previously been the Town Mead or Town Meadows, where local people had the right to pasture their cattle for six months of the year and an annual fair was held. There was early industrial enterprise at Sandford Manor, which had been used for business purposes from the mid 18th century, such as a saltpetre manufactory, and was bought in 1824 by the Imperial Gas Company who built Fulham Gas Works on the estate. Among the fine houses of the area was Peterborough House, home of the Mordaunt family, Earls of Peterborough, with more than 12 acres of grounds, and which survived until 1898.

Further north in Fulham was Walham Green, an old settlement that remained small until the

18th century, situated around the green and pond approximately where St John's church now stands. Market gardening and fruit growing became the principal activities of the area, and gradually the clusters of cottages were extended into small streets or terraces. There were a number of local inns, and the Swan Brewery was established in the 1740s. The building of St John's church in 1828 and St John's National Schools in 1836 were the start of the main period of development of Walham Green, and by the end of the 19th century it was a crowded working-class area. To the south, Eelbrook Common had been a marshy expanse of wasteland on which manorial tenants were allowed to pasture their animals, while Parsons Green was a smaller triangle of land that became a retreat for wealthy Londoners who built their houses in the vicinity. Two of the most well-known residents of Parsons Green were Mrs Fitzherbert, secret wife of the Prince of Wales (later George IV), at East End House, and Mrs Jordan, mistress of the future William IV, who lived at Belfield House.

The village of North End was slow to develop, only becoming built up in the late 19th century. The artist Sir Edward Burne-Jones moved to the Grange, North End, in 1867, and his wife described how 'there were still large elms growing in the roadway of North End, and wild roses could be gathered in a turning out of it. The space at the end of our garden was all fields.' The arrival of the District Railway in 1874 ended this country idyll. Houses were built, not only over the market gardens of the area but also the sites of several elegant houses, some of which, such as Normand House, had been schools or lunatic asylums in the early 19th century.

The heart of Hammersmith has always been the area around Queen Caroline Street, King Street and the Broadway, even before the first Hammersmith Bridge was constructed in 1827. The first church of St Paul, Hammersmith, was built in 1630-1. King Street, which was so named in about 1794, had been a turnpike since 1717 and by the mid 18th century there was already

considerable development of houses, inns and stables along the road. Boat-building, lead mills and malt houses were located around the outlet of the Stamford Brook at Hammersmith Creek, now covered by Furnival Gardens. The Creek was traversed by the High Bridge and extended as far as Cromwell's Brewery in King Street, founded in about 1780. The riverside at Hammersmith attracted wealthy residents and was lined from at least the early 18th century with fine houses, including Kent House, Westcott Lodge, Kelmscott House, Sussex House and Hammersmith Terrace, all of which survive. St Peter's Church and the handsome St Peter's Square were built in the late 1820s.

Brook Green was described by Thomas Faulkner in 1839 as 'a pleasant and respectable village embellished with several large houses'. A turnpike where travellers had to pay a toll stood near the junction of what are now Hammersmith Road and North End Road until 1863. Ribbon development was established along the main road to London by the beginning of the 19th century, and landmarks included the old workhouse on the site of Shortlands, the Red Cow, an 18th century coaching inn now rebuilt and named Latymers, and St Mary's Chapel, built in 1813. Further east on the present site of Olympia lay the Vineyard Nursery, founded in about 1745 by Lewis Kennedy and James Lee and closed in 1894 after being bought for railway land.

The estate which was known as the manor of Pallingswick was situated north of King Street. It had a great house dating back at least to the 14th century that was rebuilt in the mid 18th century and renamed Ravenscourt at about the same time. Ravenscourt Park is a surviving portion of its grounds, but the house, which became a library, was destroyed during the war. Goldhawk Road was originally a Roman road, but had fallen into disuse until it was reopened as New Road in the 1830s. Starch Green was developed later than Ravenscourt; it had been a centre of commercial rabbit breeding for at least a century, and much of the area was also in use as brick fields. The

Ordnance Survey map of 1871 shows it as still largely open land.

Shepherds Bush is not much mentioned in documents until the 19th century. John Rocque's map of the 1740s shows the triangular green, which was common land, and a few buildings. The area remained rural until the mid 19th century, situated among brickfields and market gardens. Many of the nurseries and market gardens at Shepherds Bush were small. The Hammersmith and City Railway opened in 1864 to Shepherds Bush and Hammersmith, stimulating the development of the area, which in the early years of the 20th century became well known for the White City exhibition site in Wood Lane. The part of the borough that lies north of Uxbridge Road was the last to be built up. Wormwood Scrubs was wasteland, unsuitable for cultivation even after it was cleared of the ancient woodland that covered it until the 18th century. Tenants of the manor were allowed to graze their cattle and pigs on the land. In the early 19th century the Paddington branch of the Grand Junction Canal encroached on the common, and by the mid 19th century a number of railway companies had run lines across the northern part. Wormwood Scrubs Prison was built in the 1870s by convict labour. The Old Oak and White City areas remained farmland until the 20th century.

This brief description of the earlier history of Hammersmith and Fulham gives an impression of the character and appearance of the borough before the invention of photography. From then on the camera was available to record the great changes that took place, particularly in the 20 years before World War One. The photographs that have been chosen for this book tell the story of those changes.

The Rural Past

In early times the area now covered by the Borough of Hammersmith and Fulham was rural. The well-watered and drained light gravel soil was suitable for arable farming, which was the main occupation apart from riverside activities such as fishing and ferrying. The Bishop of London was the Lord of the Manor, an area which covered the whole of the present borough, and his country residence Fulham Palace had a tithe barn dating from 1654, where grain given to the Bishop in lieu of rent was stored. Pieces of land such as Town Meadows in Fulham, near the present Wandsworth Bridge, were used by the manorial tenants to pasture their animals, according to long-established rights. Wormwood Scrubs was the largest area of wasteland, or common land, belonging to the freeholders of the Manor of Fulham. A windmill stood in the vicinity of Inglethorpe Street, Fulham, from at least the 15th century until 1794.

By the 16th century there were several references in documents to orchards in Fulham, and from the 18th century onwards a local market garden industry developed to serve the London markets, made possible by fertile soils, the availability of water and manure, and the growth of roads along which goods could be carted to London. The main market gardens were in Fulham and south Hammersmith, although there were also smaller plots of land further north. This chapter contains a photograph of quite late date, about 1900, showing strawberry pickers working a market garden. The pickers may be of Irish descent, as many men and women had emigrated from Ireland and settled in Fulham in the mid 19th century, or they may be seasonal workers from Wales or Shropshire. Until about 1870 the crop was carried to London in baskets balanced on the women's heads, after which date horse-drawn vans were used. The baskets held up to 40lbs of fruit, and the women started off in

groups at about midnight, resting their loads on stone tables provided for the purpose at various points along the road. The market gardens declined rapidly in the late 19th century as the land became increasingly valuable for building purposes and was sold to developers and covered with streets of housing.

In 1651 the writer Samuel Hartlib noted that Fulham was one of three premier regions in England for gardening. The famous gardens at Fulham Palace, planted by Bishops such as Henry Compton (1632-1713) who imported rare plants and trees, encouraged local interest in horticulture, then a comparatively new trade. By 1853 more than half of the total area of the parish of Fulham was devoted to market and nursery gardens. These included the Fulham Nursery, founded in 1700 at Hurlingham. In 1740 the owner, Christopher Gray, published a 56-page catalogue of plants, and the nursery continued under different proprietors until it was sold in the 1890s for building land. The Versailles Nursery, in West Kensington, only existed between 1848 and 1869, when some of the land was needed for the construction of the Metropolitan Railway, but was famous for the quality of its chrysanthemums, fuchsias and pansies. Its proprietor John Salter had lived in France, and introduced many new plants from abroad. Nearby was the famous Vineyard Nursery in Hammersmith Road, now the site of Olympia, founded by Lewis Kennedy and James Lee in about 1745. James Lee was a Scotsman who corresponded with Linnaeus and knew Sir Joseph Banks. He grew seeds and plants from all over the world, including 135 plants new to this country, and was the first nurseryman to make the fuchsia commercially available. By the late 19th century this nursery also had been largely swallowed up by the railway and new houses, and it finally closed in 1894.

Many of the borough's farms survived well into

the age of photography, such as Crabtree Farm and Broom Farm, featured in this chapter. Some farms grew market garden produce, for example Crabtree Farm where the Matyear family grew potatoes, onions, seakale and strawberries. Soon after 1910 the farm was sold to the developers Allen and Norris who used the land to build houses and wharves. Broom Farm, which later became the site of South Park in Fulham, was in fact a nursery garden, and in the 18th century the Rench family grew many exotic plants there, including arbutus trees, variegated hollies and the first pine strawberry to be grown in England. Nathaniel Rench, who may have introduced the red moss rose from Italy, had 35 children and died in 1783 at the age of 101 years. Grove Farm, in Bagley's Lane, had a large orchard of fruit trees and bushes in the mid 19th century. The Bagley family, who gave their name to Bagley's Lane, had several farms in the Fulham area, and were described as 'kings of Fulham'. In the north of the borough, the soil was poorer and clayey, and

farming land near Wormwood Scrubs consisted of poor quality grazing and arable that tended to be let and sub-let. Farms in this vicinity included Old Oak, also known as Wormholt Wood, and Eynhams. Both Wormwood Scrubs Prison and the White City exhibition site were built on former farmland. The area around Wormwood Scrubs did not become built up until after World War One.

London households received their milk from urban dairies, and the occupation 'cow keeper' occurs in a number of the 19th century census returns for Hammersmith and Fulham. Glover's Dairy, in Brook Green Road (now Shepherds Bush Road), for example, supplied local families with milk until about 1928, when it was replaced by Express Dairies. In the days before refrigerators, the Aylesbury Dairy at 172 Goldhawk Road offered three daily deliveries to customers. Milk was also sold in the streets from milk churns on carts, to customers who brought their own jugs to be filled.

This illustration appeared in the Illustrated London News *of 6 April 1861, captioned 'Bunching and carting carrots at Fulham'. A market garden industry developed from the early 17th century in Fulham, due to the area's fertile soils and its proximity to London. The work required a large number of seasonal labourers as can be seen by the seven individuals here employed on one task.*

Old Oak Common Lane ran north through open fields of poor quality grazing and arable land that skirted Wormwood Scrubs on the borough's western boundary. The area only began to be developed in the early 20th century. This photograph, taken around the 1890s, depicts its rural character. The low roofs of piggeries and other farm buildings flank the pond.

A family group in their Sunday best walking along Old Oak Road, near the junction of East Acton Lane, in the early 1900s. The trees and the unmade road are remnants of the countryside that have almost disappeared. The major residential development of this area occurred in the period after World War One, linked to the construction of the Westway.

This photograph, taken about 1896 from what is now the junction of Nella and Rannoch Roads, shows Crabtree House and farm buildings from Crabtree Alley. The alley originally ran through fields from Fulham Palace Road to the river. By 1894 new roads such as Wingrave, Petley and Rainville were being laid out and the urbanisation of the Crabtree area was imminent.

Crabtree Farm originally formed part of the estate of the Bishop of London. In 1804 the farm was leased to George Matyear whose family farmed the land until 1910. Potatoes, onions, seakale and strawberries were among the crops grown for the London markets. One of the carts used to transport the produce is shown in a photograph of 1896. At this time 15 men and 12 women were employed permanently, with five extra men being taken on in the spring. Edward Matyear, posing here with his horse and dog in 1900, was Crabtree's last farmer. He lived frugally and grew sweet peas as a hobby. On his death he left his estate to the King Edward VII Hospital Fund who sold it for £60,000 to the local builders Allen and Norris for housing development.

A late example of horticulture in the Wandsworth Bridge area of Fulham showing women strawberry pickers around 1900. A significant portion of the labour force had emigrated from Ireland and settled in Fulham, while others came each year from Wales and Shropshire. To avoid bruising the delicate fruit, the crop was carried to London in baskets balanced on the women's heads, a practice that continued until the 1870s.

Staff posing outside the Aylesbury Dairy at 172 Goldhawk Road in 1908. Measuring jugs used to ladle out milk from the churn hang on the side rail of the middle cart. It is interesting to see that the dairy offered three daily deliveries to customers; without domestic refrigeration fresh produce such as milk had a very short shelf life. The dairy also sold bread baked at Chibnall's bakery in Hammersmith.

Despite its name, Broom Farm, also known as Southfield Farm, on the east side of Peterborough Road, was a nursery garden. From 1711 it was in the possession of the Rench family, noted gardeners who grew many exotic plants, including tulip trees and variegated hollies. In 1870 the Veitch family, renowned nurserymen of Chelsea, acquired the property as trial grounds for plants. The photographs of the house and buildings were taken around 1900 prior to the sale of the farm and land to Fulham Borough Council for use as a public recreation ground. South Park, which was officially opened in May 1904, maintained contact with its nursery origins, since greenhouses remained on the site and parts of the park were set aside for the cultivation of flowers for municipal use.

Many London households received their milk from urban dairies, and the occupation of cow keeper occurs in a number of the 19th-century census returns for Hammersmith and Fulham. Glover's Dairy, shown here with laden delivery carts in 1910, was situated at 15 Brook Green Road (now Shepherds Bush Road). Walter Glover, the dairy manager, is wearing the straw boater. Note the wheelbarrow loaded with bedding straw and the free-range hens. In 1928 the Express Dairy Company purchased the property, part of which had been sold earlier for the construction of the Hammersmith Palais. The wall of the Palais can be seen in the background of the 1929 photograph.

Riverside

The borough's position on the River Thames has given it advantages in industry, leisure and residential opportunities. Fulham Bridge was the first bridge to be built upstream between London Bridge and Kingston, and Hammersmith Bridge, survivor of three bomb attacks, is a distinctive feature of the borough.

Fulham Bridge, built in 1729, was a narrow wooden bridge constructed by a private company and funded by the tolls that were levied on foot passengers and horse-drawn vehicles. In the 1730s tolls varied from 2s for a coach and six horses, to 6d for a score of sheep being driven across, and ½d for a foot passenger (but 1d on Sundays). The tolls became increasingly unpopular and were abolished in 1880. By that time the bridge could not cope with the greater volume of traffic that was passing across it, so between 1882-6 a new granite bridge called Putney Bridge, designed by the great Victorian engineer Sir Joseph Bazalgette, was built immediately to the west of Fulham Bridge. Putney Bridge was widened in 1933. The other bridge in Fulham, Wandsworth Bridge, was opened in 1873. Initially a toll bridge, it was declared toll-free in 1880. It too has been replaced by a newer structure, built in 1940.

Hammersmith Bridge was built in 1827, a century after Fulham Bridge. The first Hammersmith Bridge was a suspension bridge designed by William Tierney Clark, engineer to the West Middlesex Water Company in Upper Mall, who also built the chain bridge across the Danube at Budapest. Hammersmith Bridge, which was a toll bridge until 1880, was constructed by the Bird family, the most prominent 19th-century firm of builders in Hammersmith. When the old bridge became inadequate for its traffic it was replaced in 1887 by a bridge designed by Bazalgette, but unfortunately this structure is not robust enough now for heavy vehicles to use it. Hammersmith Bridge has been bombed three times by terrorists. The first attack, in 1939, caused damage to the piers although a passer-by picked up the suitcase containing the bomb and threw it over the parapet; a second bomb in 1996 was discovered before it went off, but in 2000 a third exploded and caused enough damage for the bridge to be closed again for several months.

The building of bridges across the Thames stimulated riverside development. Before this there were traditional activities along the waterfront, such as ferries plying across the river, fishing and growing beds of osiers. Some remaining farmland and the grounds of fine houses ran down to the river, but these had mostly gone by the end of the 19th century. Such houses included Brandenburgh House near Hammersmith Bridge, demolished in 1822, and Pryors Bank, Thames Bank and Willow Bank near Putney Bridge, all pulled down in the 1880s and 1890s as a result of changes and redevelopment in that area. However there also have been some notable survivals on the river. Hurlingham House, which enjoyed royal patronage, was a popular resort for sports such as pigeon shooting in the 19th century. The polo for which it was famous was discontinued in 1939, but it remains an exclusive members' club for tennis and croquet. The grounds of Fulham Palace, opened to the public as Bishops Park in 1893, offer an enjoyable stretch of river views near Putney Bridge. In Hammersmith there is a relatively unbroken frontage of surviving old houses in Lower and Upper Malls and Hammersmith Terrace.

West of Hammersmith Bridge lay the Creek, where the Stamford Brook ran into the Thames. Industries such as boat building and gas engineering were located there, as well as streets of poor housing known as Little Wapping, until the creek was filled in 1936 and Furnival Gardens was built on the site after the war. Below

Hammersmith Bridge the smell of the Hammersmith Distillery and the Manbré and Garton sugar refinery must have been pungent a century ago. The first Fulham Bridge was built before the heyday of industrial growth, but both its 19th century replacement and Wandsworth Bridge attracted the building of wharves to which goods were brought by barge. Further east there was substantial industrial development along Townmead Road on reclaimed marshy land as far as the coal wharves of Chelsea Creek.

As the industrial concerns of the 19th and early 20th centuries have closed and moved away, so some of the riverside areas in the borough have been redeveloped mainly for housing and offices, particularly between Hammersmith and Putney Bridges. The large new buildings of the Hammersmith Embankment Office Park stand on the site of the Hammersmith Distillery, previously the Brandenburgh House estate. A little further along at Palace Wharf there is a complex consisting of the River Café, the Richard Rogers Architects Partnership office and Thames Reach, a block of flats designed by Richard Rogers and built in 1985-8. Other housing on this stretch of the Thames is in local authority ownership, and a path now enables people to walk along the river. West of Putney Bridge land is becoming available as some industries depart; a Sainsburys superstore has been built on the site of Fulham Power Station, and more housing is planned. At the eastern end of the borough the exclusive Chelsea Harbour development, which was built in the late 1980s, includes flats, a hotel, restaurants and other amenities, while the former industrial basin has been converted into a marina.

Until 1729 anyone wishing to cross the Thames between Fulham and Putney had to travel by ferry. Despite opposition from watermen and other vested interests, an Act of Parliament was passed in 1726 allowing a bridge to be built. This print of 1750 shows a view of All Saints Church and Fulham High Street from the wooden structure of Fulham Bridge.

When Hammersmith Bridge, designed by William Tierney Clark, was opened in October 1827 it caused a sensation. It was an instant attraction and many people made special excursions to marvel at this first suspension bridge over the Thames. Tierney Clark went on to design other bridges, his greatest achievement being the suspension bridge over the Danube at Budapest.

An artist's romanticised impression of life on the late 19th-century river. A boat awaits the high tide at a riverside wharf on the Putney bank. In front of the tower of All Saints Church is the pseudo-Gothic residence of Pryors Bank, and to the right is Thames Bank. Both houses were demolished at the end of the 19th century.

Fulham Bridge was owned by a private company that levied charges on every pedestrian, animal and vehicle that crossed the bridge. Only the Bishop of London and his household were exempt as they travelled to and from Fulham Palace. Tolls were abolished in June 1880 to general rejoicing. This photograph of the large tollhouse at the Fulham side was taken around that time.

Before the construction of the Thames embankments, the river was shallower and froze over during exceptionally harsh winters. This view of Fulham Bridge was taken in the great frost of January 1881 when the old wooden bridge was nearing the end of its existence. In 1882 work began on a new stone bridge to the west of the old one. The designer was the distinguished civil engineer, Sir Joseph Bazalgette.

Bazalgette was also responsible for the new suspension bridge at Hammersmith, opened in 1887. His insistence on using the finest materials and workmanship was well founded as, despite bombing and increasing traffic, the bridge still stands. Here horse-drawn and motor vehicles, bicyclists and pedestrians cross from Barnes in about 1902. Houses in Lower Mall can be seen on the left.

Behind the broad span of Hammersmith Bridge in the 1950s can be seen the chimneys of riverside industries including Manbré & Garton's sugar refinery and Hammersmith Distillery. Fifty years later Charing Cross Hospital dominates the same view. To the left of the bridge The Rutland Hotel in Lower Mall sports a large flagpole.

A panoramic view of Fulham in the 1960s. Increased road traffic resulted in Putney Bridge being widened in the 1930s, removing a small piece of All Saints churchyard and most of the vicarage garden. The housing development Swan Court and, behind it, the offices of the ICL computer company, are shown under construction. This office block has now been converted into a hotel.

A view of Putney Bridge and oasthouses at Swan Wharf taken from the tower of St Mary's Church. Beside the Grand Theatre a mock Tudor arch, erected to celebrate King Edward VII's coronation, provides a temporary formal entrance to Fulham from the bridge. The Prince and Princess of Wales passed through this arch en route *to the King's Dinner to the Poor held at Bishop's Park on 5 July 1902.*

Passengers on a riverboat view a dramatic fire at Queens Wharf during the 1950s. The Caroline Estate, a block of which can be seen on the right in front of St Paul's Church tower, was built over much of this site. By the slipway are the engineering works of Rosser and Russell, established there between 1874 and 1993. The City Arms public house stands next to the bridge.

Major changes in riverside land use are graphically illustrated in the area bounded by Chelsea Creek and Basin. The triangular 19-acre site was a main shunting yard for coal trucks supplying the Fulham Power Station and the Fulham Gas Works. Coal also arrived at the site by boat. Lots Road Power Station, seen in the top photograph in 1922, provided electricity for London Underground until 2001 when it ceased operation, bringing to an end heavy industry in this area. Chelsea Harbour, a model of which is shown bottom, was developed between 1986–9, and featured a number of modern architectural styles designed to attract people to this 'instant riverside town'. Over 500 dwellings were constructed together with a hotel, restaurants and other amenities. The former industrial basin was converted into a marina.

Palace Wharf was constructed in 1907, although industrial activity began on the site as early as the 1790s. The firm of George Jackson & Son Ltd, decorative plasterers, whose work included the interior of the Lyric Theatre, was based there between 1934 and 1988. The top photograph taken in 1972 illustrates the last years of the industrial river. Sugar refiners Manbré & Garton, whose chimneys can be seen to the left of Duckham's oil refinery storage tanks, closed in 1978. By 2001, bottom, major changes have occurred. Behind Palace Wharf there is now the distinctive curved roof of the Richard Rogers Architects Partnership office.

Following the demise of riverside industry and the demolition of its associated buildings, the riverfront beyond Palace Wharf towards Hammersmith Bridge now consists mainly of property constructed within the last 25 years. These photographs, taken in 2001, show the Richard Rogers Architects Partnership office at Thames Wharf in more detail, as well as Thames Reach, a block of flats designed by Richard Rogers and built in 1985–8. The steel balconies are designed to suggest a nautical theme, reminiscent of the deck of a ship, linking the flats to the river below. A riverside path has been constructed for this stretch of the Thames.

The presence of the advertising and marketing company WWAV Rapp Collins Media in the newly built Hammersmith Embankment Office Park highlights the shift in employment from manufacturing to service industries in the borough. This photograph, taken in 2001, shows the first stage of a major office development on the site of the former Manbré and Garton sugar refining factory.

Transport

The development of the transport infrastructure has been a key factor in the growth of Hammersmith and Fulham as an inner London suburb. The area was always characterised by its position on the river and on main routes leading westwards out of London, affecting it socially and economically. Until the early 19th century people got about by means of stagecoaches for longer distances, hackney coaches for shorter journeys, and riverboats and ferries. Goods were transported by horse and cart, and wealthy people kept their own carriages and horses in private stables. In 1825 there were 24 coaches travelling from the city of London to the borough, making a total of 58 return journeys per day. Although coaches could pick up and set down passengers, many of their seats were pre-booked, and it wasn't until horse-drawn omnibuses were introduced to London by George Shillibeer in 1829 that a more convenient and flexible way of travelling was provided.

Bus services rapidly expanded, and by 1840 a number of bus proprietors were listed in a local directory of Hammersmith. The London General Omnibus Company, formed in 1855, and its later rival the London Road Car Company (1880), gradually took over the smaller private enterprises. Some of the bus journeys were surprisingly similar to, if not better than, today's in terms of time and frequency; for example, in 1888 it was possible to take a bus from Hammersmith to Liverpool Street every 4 minutes, and the journey took about 70 minutes. The fare was 4d (about 1½ p). After World War One horses were replaced by the petrol-driven bus, and some of the bodies for the LGOC buses were made at coach works in Olaf Street and Seagrave Road. In 1923 the LGOC were operating 23 motorbus routes, of which several ran through the borough, including the No. 9, which is one of London's oldest. The formation of the London Passenger Transport Board in 1933 signalled the end of the remaining independent bus companies that had been operating rather chaotically.

From 1861 onwards an alternative form of travel in London was offered by trams, which gave a smoother ride and could carry more passengers than buses. The first section of tramway in the area opened in 1874 along Uxbridge Road, and there were soon several tram companies. By 1910 the London County Council, which had a tram depot in Great Church Lane (now Talgarth Road), had bought up most of the tramlines in London. Shepherds Bush and Hammersmith had the earliest electrified routes in the capital, introduced in 1901. Trams ran from 1909 onwards down Fulham Palace Road, but never operated in central Fulham because the streets in Walham Green were too narrow. In the 1930s the new London Passenger Transport Board began to convert tramways to trolleybus operation. Trolleybuses were easier to maintain because they did not run on tracks, and could pull into the kerb to pick up passengers. Several routes in the borough were converted, but World War Two stopped the process, and in 1946 it was announced that in future trams would be replaced by diesel buses rather than trolleybuses.

Overground railways first arrived when the West London Railway/West London Extension Railway opened fully in 1862-3, running approximately along the eastern boundary of the borough from Fulham up through White City and Wormwood Scrubs to Willesden Junction. Several stations on the line closed in 1940 and never reopened, including Chelsea and Fulham, Uxbridge Road, and St Quintin Park and Wormwood Scrubs. The London and South Western Railway ran a line from Richmond to Waterloo, opened in 1869, via stations at Shepherds Bush and Hammersmith (The Grove) which were demolished after the railway ceased operation in 1916. Various lines crossed the area of Hammersmith north of Old Oak Common, which became a tangle of railway tracks, sidings and junctions. The North Pole Depot, which is used by Eurostar trains, lies within the borough adjacent to Scrubs Lane.

The underground is an essential part of the local transport network. Fulham is served only by the District Line (formerly the Metropolitan District Railway), which was extended to Hammersmith via West Kensington in 1874, and to Putney Bridge in 1880. Some existing railway stations were used, while others such as Barons Court (1905) and Stamford Brook (1912) were added later. Hammersmith is accessible via several tube lines. The Hammersmith and City Railway (now the Hammersmith and City line of the Metropolitan Railway) was extended to Hammersmith in 1864. Shepherds Bush and Goldhawk Road Stations were built in 1914, but Wood Lane Station closed in the same year except for occasional use for events at the White City. The first modern deep tube railway was the Central London Railway, nicknamed the Twopenny Tube and later renamed the Central

Line, which opened eastward from Shepherds Bush in 1900 and westwards in 1920. The Piccadilly Line opened from Hammersmith to Finsbury Park in 1906, and was extended to Uxbridge and Hounslow West in 1933 and to Heathrow in 1977, creating a fast link to the airport that has encouraged business development in Hammersmith.

The 20th century saw enormous growth in the use of motor vehicles, which meant that new roads and traffic systems had to be built to accommodate the flow of traffic along the western London routes. A major road out of London had been planned since World War One, and the Hammersmith Flyover, which carries the A4 through central Hammersmith, was finally opened in 1961 a few years after the Great West Road was driven through the area south of King Street. Further north, the Westway between White City and Paddington and the first section of the West Cross Route opened in 1970. In Fulham, where most streets are narrow and there was never much opportunity to enlarge existing roads, the problem of traffic congestion will be a challenge for the 21st century.

A horse-drawn cab stands outside Hammersmith station, Beadon Road, in 1894. The station, now the terminus of the Hammersmith and City line, was reconstructed with a brick façade in 1908. Stafford's, the shop next to the station, repaired and sold umbrellas. The hansom cab was the Victorian equivalent of a taxi. By 1904 seven and a half thousand licensed hansoms were plying for hire in London.

From 1869 the London and South Western Railway ran services between Kensington and Richmond via Shepherds Bush and Hammersmith (The Grove) stations, in a loop joining up with the existing District Line. Intended to link Richmond with the city, this roundabout route lost out to the more direct electrified District Line and was closed to passengers in 1916. This postcard hints at the leisurely tempo of trains using the line.

Hammersmith (The Grove) station was opened in 1869. Situated near the junction of Glenthorne Road, north of the present Hammersmith and City Line station, it was built on an embankment 20 feet above ground level. Although close to Hammersmith Broadway, its general appearance was that of a rural station. The station was closed to passengers in 1916 and the Wimpey office block subsequently occupied the site.

Willesden Junction Station, in the extreme north of the borough, was opened in 1866 to serve a number of railway lines that converged at this point. These cabs waiting in about 1905 could expect passengers from major northern cities as well as local stations, including those on the West London Railway. This line has recently become more significant, with an increased service and the reopening of West Brompton station.

Shepherds Bush Station on the London and South Western Railway opened in 1874 at the northern end of Shepherds Bush Road. Although the line closed in 1916 the remains of the station can still be seen in this photograph of 1949. Across the road are Shepherds Bush Baptist Tabernacle and The Grampians flats. Sulgrave Gardens flats were erected on the station site around 1957.

The London and South Western Railway line crossed Beadon Road by a bridge and on to a viaduct. The local firm, George Cohen Sons & Co, was contracted to dismantle the bridge in 1956. This had to be done at night after the last trolley bus had passed under the arch at 11.45pm. The surviving viaduct piers run parallel to the District Line, north of the King's Mall shopping centre.

HART'S
WEST LONDON RAILWAY
UXBRIDGE ROAD
STATION
LOCKHARTS.
DINNERS TEAS

The West London Railway, after an unsuccessful brief earlier existence, re-opened for passenger services in 1862. The entrance to Uxbridge Road Station, seen here about 1914, is flanked by dining establishments, including Lockharts, who had a number of outlets in the borough. Beyond the station stands the ornate turret of the Royal Hotel. These buildings were demolished to make way for the West Cross Route roundabout.

Shops selling familiar products such as fruit, hosiery, tobacco and newspapers, line the booking hall of the Hammersmith Metropolitan District Railway station in June 1928. Two years later work began on the western extension of the Piccadilly Line, and the station was reconstructed to accommodate the increase in passenger numbers. (Reproduced by kind permission of London's Transport Museum.)

The Central London Railway, the capital's first deep-level electric tube line, was opened in 1900, linking west London with the city at Bank. As this photograph of Shepherds Bush station in 1901 shows, the company set a flat fare of 2d, leading to the nickname 'the Twopenny Tube'. The line was extended to Wood Lane in 1908 for access to the White City exhibition grounds.

At the Parsons Green depot of the London Passenger Transport Board craftsmen construct the familiar signs seen at all underground stations. The chief executive officer of the Board, Frank Pick, was responsible for the promotion of good design standards. The timeless, legible and simple forms of the typeface were designed in 1916 by the Hammersmith calligrapher Edward Johnston. This view of the workshop was taken in 1933. (Reproduced by kind permission of London's Transport Museum.)

Walham Green station opened in 1880 when the Metropolitan District Railway extended its line from West Brompton to Putney Bridge. Six years later the railway crossed the river south to Wimbledon. Advertisements for various destinations served by the railway's successor, the District Line, can be seen on the hoardings above the station buildings. The date of the postcard is contemporary with the conversion from steam to electric traction on the line in 1905. The elegant façade of the station, rebuilt in 1910, shows clearly in the modern photograph. Walham Green remained the name of the station until 1952 when, after representations from the Fulham Chamber of Commerce, it was changed to Fulham Broadway. The scene in 2001 shows part of the major redevelopment on the north side of the Broadway under construction.

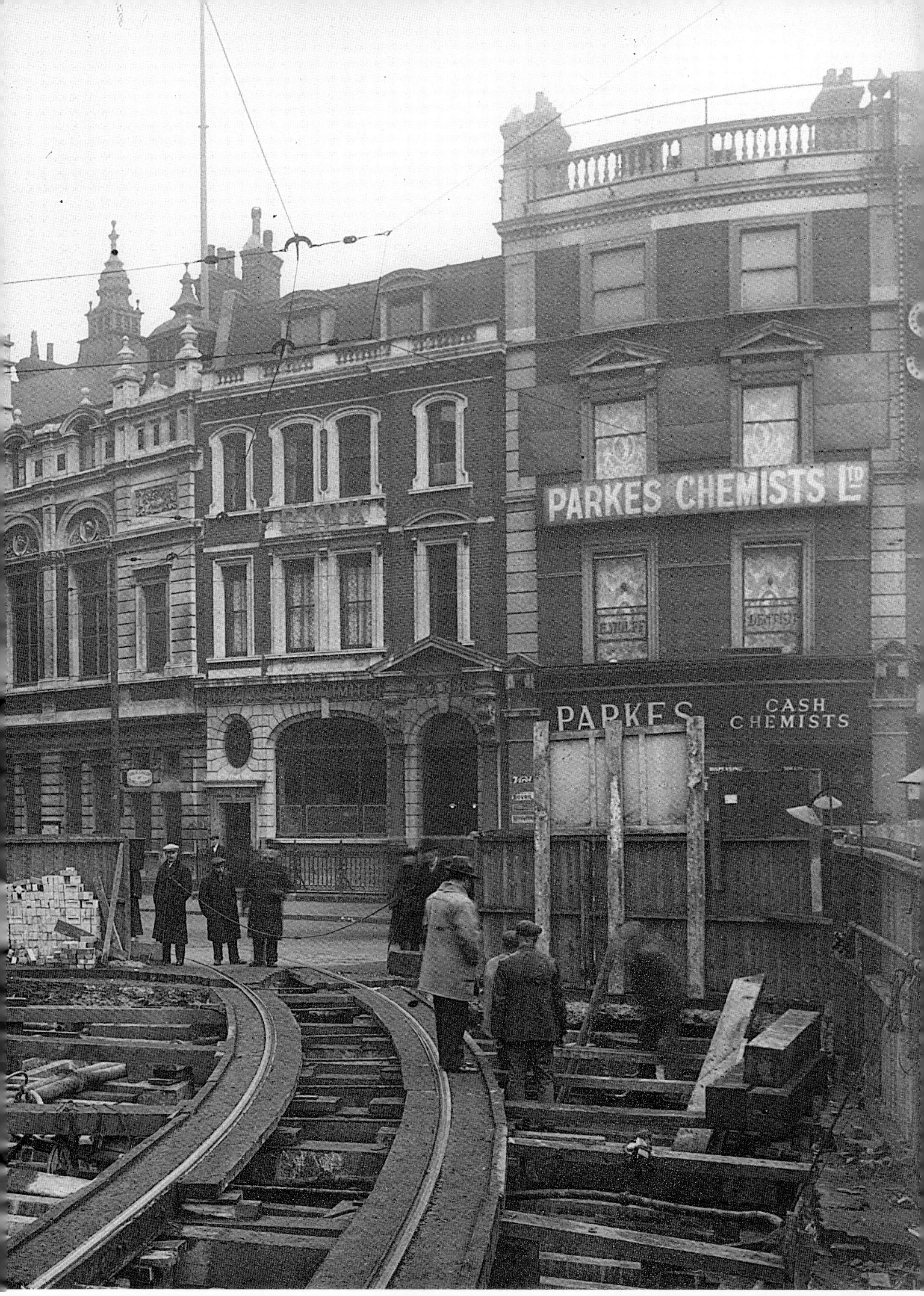
PARKES CHEMISTS Ltd
PARKES
CASH CHEMISTS
DENTIST

Above and previous page: In 1930 work began on a westward extension of the Piccadilly Line reaching Uxbridge and Hounslow West by 1933. Both these photographs show the work in progress early in 1931. Hammersmith station was rebuilt to include a subway linking it with the north side of the Broadway. A tram waits outside Hammersmith Town Hall in Brook Green Road (now Shepherds Bush Road) for clearance to travel over the construction site. North-west of the Broadway, the Piccadilly Line passed under Beadon Road to run parallel with the District Line tracks. Market stalls can be seen at the end of Bradmore Grove beyond the original Lyric Theatre. The Kings Mall shopping development, incorporating the rebuilt Lyric Theatre, now occupies this site. (Reproduced by kind permission of London's Transport Museum.)

Railway track and points were made at the large running and maintenance depot at Lillie Bridge, West Kensington. Stacked railway sleepers can be seen in the foreground of this photograph taken in April 1931. Behind the depot stand William Whiteley's depositories and laundry. In later years the depot manufactured 300ft fixed rail lengths for the underground. (Reproduced by kind permission of London's Transport Museum.)

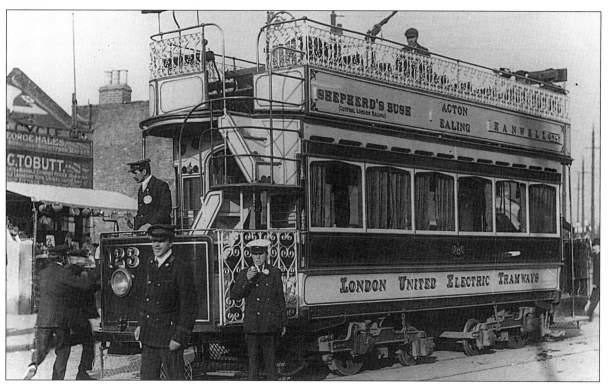

Shepherds Bush and Hammersmith had the first electrified tramway routes in London. The London United Tramways Company introduced electrification using power from overhead cables on their routes in 1901. A type X No.123 tram is shown with its crew at Shepherds Bush in about 1905. Trams were replaced by more versatile trolleybuses in the 1930s.

Trolleybuses in Hammersmith Grove in October 1935. This road is now the pedestrianised Lyric Square. The tram track turning into Beadon Road can be seen in the foreground. To the right is Lawson's drapers shop in Grove Hall and next to it is the Sun Life Insurance office with its sun emblem over the door. The Hop Poles public house in King Street is visible behind the further trolleybus.

The entrance to Hammersmith bus garage in Talgarth Road, May 1972. The garage was built by the London General Omnibus Company in 1913 and occupied the south-west corner of what is now the Broadway Centre. Beyond the garage is the brick building of the Britannia public house. In the background construction is underway on the Cunard International Hotel, now the Novotel complex.

Public Buildings

As the population of Hammersmith and Fulham increased during the 19th century, new amenities were needed to meet people's educational, spiritual, health and leisure needs. Schools, churches, hospitals, theatres, cinemas and even prisons were built in the borough and some of this legacy survives today.

The parish of Fulham formerly covered the whole of the present borough, although from 1631 Hammersmith had its own chapel of ease, St Paul's Church. In 1834 the parish of Hammersmith was created, and in 1836 St Peter's Church, built in 1829, was also given its own parish. From then on a number of other parishes were formed and new churches erected to cope with the growing size of congregations. The two old churches of the borough, All Saints, Fulham and St Paul, Hammersmith, were both rebuilt in much larger form in the early 1880s. Inevitably, as religious observance dwindled during the 20th century, a time came when churches and chapels had to be made redundant, and some, such as St Clement, Fulham Palace Road, were demolished. Others, for example St Augustine, Lillie Road, were not rebuilt after wartime bombing, but St Katherine, Westway (1959) and St Mary, Hammersmith Road (1961) were restored in more modern form. Sometimes a place of worship has changed denomination; the Fulham and Kensington Synagogue at 259 Lillie Road, built in 1927, became a Seventh Day Adventist Church.

There have been changes also in the borough's schools, as well as some notable examples of continuity. Until the Education Act of 1870 introduced state education, schooling was provided by church and charity schools, as well as a number of privately run schools, both day and boarding. The small private schools have disappeared, but some well-known larger schools with private or charitable origins survive, for example Latymer Upper School in King Street, opened in 1895 with funding from Edward Latymer's charitable bequest of 1624. St Paul's School was situated in Hammersmith Road between 1884 and 1968, after which it moved to Barnes and its massive range of Alfred Waterhouse buildings were demolished. Its sister school, St Paul's Girls' School in Brook Green, opened in 1904, still flourishes, as does Godolphin and Latymer Girls' School in Iffley Road, opened in 1906. Generations of children were educated at church primary schools prior to the 1870 Act. Some were of ancient origin, such as All Saints School, now in Bishops Avenue, which was probably founded in 1610. Many church schools have moved or been rebuilt, for example St Paul's Church of England Primary School, which had to be reconstructed in 1958 when its site was needed for the A4 flyover. Among other state schools there has also been a pattern of rebuilding and mergers, particularly as some were affected by wartime bombing.

The borough has two notable hospitals. Hammersmith Hospital developed from the Hammersmith Workhouse Infirmary, built in 1905 in Du Cane Road, which was thought to be so luxurious that it was nicknamed the Paupers' Paradise. After wartime use as a military hospital it was administered from 1930 onwards as a teaching hospital, specialising in orthopaedics and plastic surgery. The Fulham Workhouse Infirmary was erected in Fulham Palace Road in 1883-4, and developed into a general hospital in the years before 1914. The name was changed to Fulham Hospital in 1928, and despite bomb damage on several occasions it remained open during World War Two. Fulham Hospital was amalgamated with Charing Cross Hospital in 1959, and a large new hospital called Charing Cross Hospital was opened in 1973. Other hospitals in the borough included the Western Hospital, Seagrave Road, which originally opened as a smallpox hospital in

1877; it was closed in 1979 and the site is now covered by housing. West London Hospital in Hammersmith Road, founded in 1856 and closed in 1993, was the first hospital in England to install X-ray equipment, in 1921. The façade has survived during its recent conversion to offices. The 1930s architecture of the Royal Masonic Hospital in Ravenscourt Park, now a private hospital called the Stamford, is also still intact.

As local government developed throughout the 19th century, halls were erected to serve as the headquarters first of the vestries, and after 1900 of the Metropolitan Boroughs. Fulham Town Hall, which is a Grade II-listed building with a Portland stone façade, was designed by George Edwards and built for Fulham Vestry in 1888-90. An extension facing Harwood Road was added in 1904-5 by Francis Wood, the Borough Engineer. Old Hammersmith Town Hall, in the Broadway, was opened in 1897 and not pulled down until 1962, although it had been superseded in 1939 by the present Town Hall in King Street, designed by E. Berry Webber. The future of the extension that was added to the Town Hall in 1971–5 is currently under review.

Photographs of a few of the theatres and cinemas of the borough are included in this chapter, a record of the expansion of public places of entertainment that took place until World War Two. The Lyric Theatre in King Street, first opened in 1888, still exists within a late-1970s structure, retaining much of its Victorian plasterwork interior. The Grand Theatre at Putney Bridge and the Granville Theatre of Varieties at Walham Green were demolished in 1958 and 1971 respectively. The King's Theatre and the Hammersmith Palace have also gone, but the Shepherds Bush Empire, opened in 1903 as a music hall, is now a venue for rock concerts. In the early 1900s there were several cinemas in both Fulham and Hammersmith, some of them short-lived, and others were built in the 1920s and 30s. All have closed and been demolished or turned into bingo halls or other uses, such as the Gaumont Palace Cinema in Hammersmith, which is now the Apollo, a venue for live theatre and concerts.

The UGC in King Street (formerly the Regal), for some years the only functioning cinema in the borough, has been joined by a Warner Village Cinema complex at Shepherds Bush Green, opened in February 2002.

The first St Paul's Church, consecrated in 1631, was a chapel-of-ease for Hammersmith residents who lived in the northern part of the parish of Fulham, which covered the whole area of the present borough. The church was enlarged in 1864 and this photograph, looking west from the junction of Queen Street and Great Church Lane, was taken sometime after that date. The present church was built in 1883.

Demolition commences on the roof of the Broadway Congregational Church in 1923. The church was pulled down as part of the widening of the southern end of Brook Green Road (Shepherds Bush Road). The congregation moved to a new church opposite, which was replaced by offices in 1979. With the exception of Hammersmith Fire Station, at the extreme right, all the buildings depicted here have disappeared.

St Mary's Church was built as another chapel-of-ease to All Saints, Fulham, in 1814. It was situated on the south side of King Street East (later Hammersmith Road). The church was enlarged in 1884 to meet the increase in population and St Mary's later became a parish in its own right. This view of the Victorian gothic interior, showing the chancel, choir and organ, dates from about 1918. The church was destroyed by a flying bomb on 16 July 1944. Services were held at St Mary's Mission Hall in North End Road until the consecration in 1961 of the new church, designed by Lord Mottistone and Paul Paget. The striking tower is well illustrated in this photograph of 1968.

A bombing raid on 14 September 1940
destroyed St Catherine Coleman Church,
Westway. The church, designed by Robert
Atkinson, was barely 20 years old,
having been consecrated in 1923. On VE
day (8 May 1945), a service of
thanksgiving was held in the ruins.

In 1958 a new church, designed by the son of the original architect, was built on the foundations of the former St Catherine Coleman and renamed St Katherine. The surviving communion rails, which had originally come from St Katherine Coleman, Fenchurch Street, were installed in a side chapel. In 1979 the building was converted to include a community centre. Statues of Saints Catherine, Michael and Andrew look out over the Westway in the photograph of 2001.

St John's National School, built in 1836, was situated at Walham Green on a triangle of land bounded by Vanston Place, Jerdan Place and Fulham Road. St John's Church tower is shown in the background of this sketch. The school has moved twice since 1894 and now occupies the former Munster Road School site in Filmer Road.

An infant class at Peterborough School, Clancarty Road, celebrating May Day in 1903. The school opened in 1901 and began to admit pupils with physical disabilities in 1905. Peterborough School was also used by the congregation of Christ Church for services until 1903 when the church was consecrated.

In his will of 1624 Edward Latymer left funds for the education of poor boys of Hammersmith. Provision was made for pupils at various parochial and private schools until, in 1863, the Latymer Foundation School was established in a new building in King Street East (Hammersmith Road). An outdoor exercise class is seen here around 1929. The school closed in 1963 and the buildings were subsequently demolished for office development.

Westville Road School, opened in 1886, was destroyed on 20 February 1944, during a night of intensive bombing in the borough. Firewatcher George Gooch and nurse Edith Guyatt, together with three residents in Westville Road, were killed in that incident. The photograph taken the following day shows the extent of the damage to the school and surrounding houses.

The rebuilt school was opened in 1952 as Westville School and is seen here two years later from the vantage point of Mark Mansions. Beyond the school is the bell turret of the former St Mary's Mission Hall. The school is now called Greenside Primary School.

St Paul's School, designed by Alfred Waterhouse, was a striking feature in Hammersmith Road from 1884. This view from the playing fields was taken in February 1969, after the school had moved to Barnes. The buildings were demolished in 1970 for the erection of flats and Hammersmith & West London College. The sale and development of the site with the loss of its open space caused great controversy.

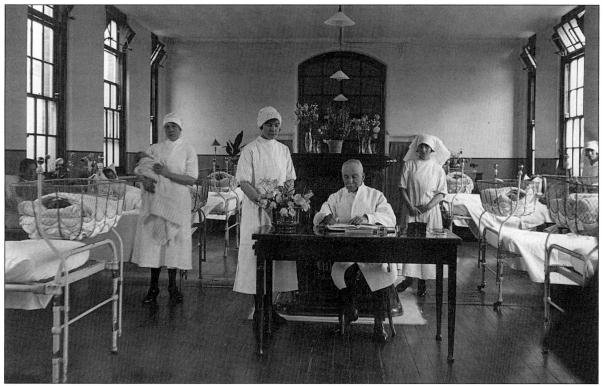

Staff in a maternity ward at Hammersmith Hospital pose with the doctor in this 1927 photograph. The cots hanging on gimbals at the end of each bed enabled the babies to be rocked to sleep. The hospital's maternity function has been strengthened in 2000 with the transfer of Queen Charlotte's Hospital from Goldhawk Road to new buildings at the Du Cane Road site.

Fulham Infirmary was built in 1872 as part of the Fulham Union workhouse. It soon proved inadequate for the area's rapidly expanding population and a new infirmary, built by the local firm of Gibbs & Flew, was opened in 1884. The old building, photographed in 1962 from Margravine Road, continued in use for chronically ill patients. It was demolished after the final closure of Fulham Hospital in 1973.

Viewed from Parfrey Street in 1979, the 14 floors of Charing Cross Hospital on the former Fulham Hospital site dominate the surrounding area. Ralph Tubbs' cruciform design permitted more natural light into the wards than could have been achieved with a rectangular structure. On opening in 1973 the building contained 630 beds. Further expansion has increased patient capacity.

A major local campaign was fought to save the West London Hospital in Hammersmith Road when it was threatened with closure in the 1980s. The hospital finally closed in 1993, but the façade of the building was preserved as a planning condition for redevelopment of the site as offices. This photograph of the newly completed building prior to occupation was taken in 2001.

This new surgery on the corner of Hammersmith Bridge Road and Sussex Place was designed by Guy Greenfield and opened in 2000. From the road the façade appears to be a blank wall but is made up of a series of stepped sections with the entrance and windows in the resulting spaces. The highly acclaimed design helps to insulate the building from the worst effects of the nearby traffic.

Fulham Women's Convict Prison, originally named Fulham Refuge, was established in Burlington Road in 1856. Its most notorious inmate was Constance Kent who confessed to the murder of her infant half-brother. The prison closed in 1888 and the site was later developed for housing. This photograph of the prison entrance was taken in 1895 just prior to demolition.

The old Vestry Hall in Fulham Road, Walham Green, was used as local government offices until increasing staff numbers and local prestige demanded a new building. Like many London vestries Fulham launched an architectural competition in the 1880s to design a grand vestry hall to provide a focus for civic identity.

After an ill-tempered competition, involving accusations of unfairness and nepotism, George Edwards' design was chosen for the new Fulham Vestry (now Town) Hall. Construction started in 1888 and took two years to complete, costing twice the amount stipulated in the rules. This 1899 print shows the magnificently proportioned Fulham Road frontage.

This photograph shows the present Hammersmith Town Hall nearing completion in 1939. Designed by E. Berry Webber it superseded the late Victorian building in Brook Green Road (Shepherds Bush Road), which was demolished in 1962. The outbreak of World War Two prevented any formal opening ceremony for the new premises.

An artist's impression of the King Street entrance to Hammersmith Town Hall under the five-storey extension, built in 1971-5. The grand staircase leading to the first floor was demolished. The original main entrance to the town hall was on the south side but, since the widening of the Great West Road, this was no longer used.

The Shepherds Bush Empire, designed by Frank Matcham, was opened in 1903 as a variety theatre seating 2,332. Members of the staff and orchestra pose in front of the building in 1905. The theatre was closed in 1953 and converted into a television theatre for the BBC. After a further closure it reopened in 1994 as a music venue. (Reproduced by kind permission of Mrs E. Fincham.)

The Star Cinema, 121 Wandsworth Bridge Road, appears resolutely closed on 12 March 1915. Among the posters can be seen the one bearing the wartime message 'Britons Your Country Needs You'. The cinema opened in December 1913 and closed finally in 1956. It was demolished in 1961 for a development of houses and shops.

Like many cinemas the Savoy, shown here in 1976, ended its life as a bingo hall. Situated at Western Circus, it was part of the suburban development that followed the construction of the Westway. The Savoy was demolished in 1996 as it stood in the path of a proposed road-widening scheme. This was subsequently abandoned leaving a strip of wasteland where once the cinema and houses lined the road.

Opened in 1902, the King's Theatre in Hammersmith Road, seen here in about 1910, was a popular venue for touring companies. Ballet and opera productions were also staged. The theatre closed in 1955 and was used as television studio for four years. It was demolished in 1963 and the site is now offices.

Streets

The suburban landscape is mainly characterised by the streets of houses that have been built to accommodate the people of a town or borough. Photographs of streets form the largest subject area in the visual collections of the Archives and Local History Centre.

The development of an area can be traced by looking at the Ordnance Survey maps, which were published every 30 years or so after the first edition of the 1860s. Before this maps are smaller-scale and less informative, although they can give an excellent overview of an area. The earliest useful map of Hammersmith and Fulham is John Rocque's map of 1741-6. It shows scattered settlements in Fulham at Walham Green, Fulham High Street and along the North End Road. The rest of the area is market gardens and fields, apart from some large houses and estates such as Peterborough House. In Hammersmith there is development along the river and in what became King Street, Queen Caroline Street, the Broadway and Hammersmith Road, but little else apart from a hamlet at Shepherds Bush. Nothing but fields and the woods of Wormwood Scrubs lie north of the Uxbridge Road. Over a century later the 6 in:1 mile Ordnance Survey map of 1874 shows remarkably little change, although development has increased in the Hammersmith Broadway area and is starting to spread along the principal streets such as Fulham Road. The OS map of 1894-6 tells a different story, as by then extensive areas of the borough have been built up with streets of houses. There is still undeveloped land along the river between Crabtree and Fulham Palace and from Putney Bridge to Chelsea Harbour, around the southern end of Fulham Palace Road and around Hurlingham, as well as in northern Hammersmith. By the time of World War One these remaining spaces have been filled in, apart from Old Oak which was only developed when the Old Oak Estate was built in the 1920s.

There were opportunities for local builders to enrich themselves during the period of rapid expansion in housing that began in the mid 19th century. In Hammersmith the Bird family were, for two generations, one of the most successful building contractors. Apart from houses, they built the first Hammersmith Bridge, St Peter's Church and buildings at the West Middlesex Water Works in Upper Mall, and were prominent in local public life. In Fulham active local builders included Jimmy Nichols, who built the Peterborough Estate in the early 1890s, the partnership of Gibbs and Flew, who teamed up in 1876 and built the Margravine, Fulham Park, Munster Park and several other residential developments, and Allen and Norris, who developed the Crabtree Farm estate before World War One. At the turn of the 20th century mansion blocks became popular in areas such as Barons Court, providing flats for those who were using the District Line and other improved transport links to commute to work.

Housing working people was a challenge that the local authorities had to meet as the population expanded and industry flourished. By the mid 19th century there were notorious slums in the area of Fulham around Fulham Fields and Walham Green, where Irish labourers working in the market gardens lived. In 1901 each house in The Avenues (Rock, Grove, Walham and Lodge Avenues, south of Heckfield Place) was occupied by 10 or 11 people, and a survey of 1931 found that nearly half the houses in Fulham, many of which lacked bathrooms, were home to more than one family. Trafalgar Street in Hammersmith, in the area known as Little Wapping near the Creek, was found to contain 213 people living in 22 houses in 1891. In the early years of the 20th century housing such as the War Seal Mansions in Fulham Road (now the Sir Oswald Stoll Mansions) and the Guinness

Trust and Peabody Estate developments at the northern end of Fulham Palace Road eased the shortage. They were followed by local authority developments, such as the Wormholt Estate, built in the early 1920s, and Fulham Court (1933). The London County Council also provided housing, including the Old Oak Estate, a cottage estate of some 1,055 dwellings built between 1912 and 1927, and the White City Estate, built in the late 1930s on land formerly occupied by part of the White City exhibition site. Clearance of the worst slums was largely complete by World War Two, and municipal housing provision became even more important after the war because so many dwellings had been destroyed or damaged. Post-war council developments included Sulivan Court, built in 1950-6 on the former polo ground at Hurlingham Club, the Clem Attlee Estate, opened in 1957, and the Edward Woods Estate on the east side of the West Cross Route, opened in the mid 1960s.

The most significant modern changes to the physical appearance of the streets of the borough are related to the improved standard of living of the late 20th century. Much of Fulham has been gentrified: houses that were formerly inhabited by the working classes have been renovated by their owners and are now fetching high prices. Expensive new houses and blocks of private flats have been erected wherever developers can find space caused by the departure of industries or institutions, for example at Chelsea Harbour and on the sites of Cadby Hall, the Western Hospital and Fulham Power Station.

Hammersmith has not been so affected by the process, particularly the more deprived northern part of the area. The constantly increasing volume of traffic has meant that many of the streets in the borough are clogged with vehicles. Some commercial developments are currently being built or planned, for example at Fulham Broadway and on a larger scale at the White City on the site of former railway land. Overall, however, the basic pattern of streets that was established in the late 19th and early 20th centuries is unlikely to be significantly altered, and there is little spare land for radical new building in the borough.

An exceptionally high tide inundated Fulham High Street in January 1877. Both Fulham and Hammersmith riverside areas were at risk from flooding on a number of occasions in the past, situated as they were on low-lying ground and unprotected by an embankment wall. This illustration of the flooded streets, and the next three photographs of the High Street, capture the spirit of the 'Old Town'.

A group of houses lining the west side of Fulham High Street, looking north, in about 1895. At that date businesses included a wheelwright, gunsmith, baker, upholsterer and farrier. In contrast to the later urban landscape of uniform terraces, these houses demonstrate individual and distinctive styles. They were replaced by Parkview Court.

Mr Benjamin Wright standing in front of old cottages at 28 & 30 Fulham High Street in about 1900. Adjoining on the left is the entrance to Mr Alfred Stammers' shop. He was listed in local directories as an oilman, but also sold a wide range of household goods, including soap, lamps, cocoa and ginger beer.

Taken about 1907 looking south down Fulham High Street this photograph also shows a corner of the Grand Theatre, at the foot of Putney Bridge. When the bridge and its approach road were opened in 1886 the southern end of the High Street inevitably became a minor thoroughfare.

The photographer leant from an upper window of 121 New Kings Road to capture the street stretching away to the south-west in about 1895. Across the road lies the tongue of land known as Fulham Common but now regarded as part of Eelbrook Common, south of Crondace Road. In 1878 the owners of the common attempted to sell it for building purposes but were routed by vociferous local protesters.

A bustling New Kings Road at the beginning of World War One looking east from Guion Road towards the trees lining Parsons Green. Motor cars share the road with horse-drawn vehicles. In the terrace on the right food shops are much in evidence, some displaying advertisements for national brands such as Hovis bread.

Shops in Fulham Road, adjacent to the Town Hall, about 1917. The Broadway Gardens Picture Theatre on the opposite side of the road screened the latest war news as advertised on the top billboard above White's oyster bar. On the extreme right of the photograph is the entrance to the White Hart public house, which remains on this site.

Fulham Road seen from the junction of Crookham Road in 1904, looking east towards the former Munster Park Methodist Church. The building was opened in 1882 and, although demolished in 1971, services continued in a smaller church on the site until 1994. The lack of vehicles, allowing pedestrians to walk in the road with impunity, is in complete contrast to the current traffic situation in the borough.

504
STOWE
CONTRACTOR
For Removals
PANTECHNICONS
COVERED VANS
By The HOUR
DAY or JOB

The junction of Fulham Road and Melmoth Place, later North End Road, Walham Green in 1896. St John's church tower can be seen in the background. Edwin Stowe, of 504 Fulham Road, who advertised as a removals contractor was also a greengrocer, as shown by the fresh produce that is being sold from the containers underneath the awnings.

The same row of shops in Fulham Road in 1962. The upper floors of 498, 502 and 504 have been demolished, leaving that of Johnnie's gramophone record shop in dilapidated isolation. Grayton House, a 1984 office development on the corner of North End Road, replaced the buildings to the left of Wheeler's motor coach booking office.

Palace Terrace, Fulham Palace Road, was built in the late 1880s on the site of four large houses known collectively as High Bank. The red brick terrace running between Lalor Street and Fulham Road overlooked the grounds of Fulham Palace. The surrounding wall can be seen to the right of the photograph, taken about 1906.

Heckfield Place formed part of the area of Fulham known as The Avenues. This 1937 photograph was one of a series taken by the council's Public Health Department to illustrate the unsuitable housing conditions. The large building in the background is the rear of the Regal Cinema in North End Road. The outbreak of World War Two delayed redevelopment plans.

The muddy surface of the unfinished roadway is very noticeable at the junction of Lillie and Fulham Palace Roads in 1893. To the left the roofline of Everington Street School rises above the houses in Bothwell and Hawksmoor Streets. On the right railings mark the boundary of the newly opened Lillie Road Recreation Ground.

Activity around the entrance to the Earls Court Exhibition grounds at the eastern end of Lillie Road, close to West Brompton Station. In July 1906 visitors passed under the illuminated archways to marvel at the sights of the Imperial Austrian Exhibition, which had opened two months earlier. Behind the terrace on the right was the large goods and coal depot of the Midland Railway.

Brompton Park Crescent was built between 1984 and 1986 as a private residential development of 300 units on the site of the former Western Hospital, Seagrave Road. As this 2001 photograph shows the landscaping design has matured around the estate, which is set within its own secured area.

These houses were built on a triangular site that now fronts Queen Caroline Street between Hammersmith Bridge Road and Blacks Road. The photograph was probably taken in the early 1930s when 16 Hammersmith Bridge Road was occupied by firms of solicitors. By 1939 Palmers department store had taken over the property which was demolished soon afterwards.

The office development on the corner of Hammersmith Road and Butterwick is typical of the contemporary urban landscape in central Hammersmith. The original Bechtel building that replaced 19th-century property on the site had a flat glass frontage but a refurbishment in 2001 added interest to the façade.

A busy junction at the corner of Queen (Caroline) Street and (Hammersmith) Bridge Road in 1896. As this was the main approach road to Hammersmith Bridge advertisement hoardings directed potential customers to prominent local businesses. At 6 Queen Street, next to the Robin Hood beerhouse, is the shop of George Tuggy, boot maker. John Nettleton in Bridge Road combined a veterinary practice with a blacksmith's shop.

King Street looking east in about 1908. The photograph was taken from what is now Nigel Playfair Avenue. In the centre of the road a passenger boards the Chiswick bound tram and the eastbound tram track can be seen turning left into Studland Street. Next to Child's fancy goods store is the low frontage of the 18th-century Cock and Magpie public house.

Looking west from the corner of Studland Street, the spire of Rivercourt Methodist Church rises over King Street in the 1920s. A cinema has stood on the site on the left for 90 years, from the Blue Hall, built in 1912, to the present UGC.

This stretch of King Street from Bridge Avenue to Hammersmith Broadway in the distance is busy with shoppers in 1922. On the pavement outside the tailors' establishment of Lockwood & Bradley a milk seller stands with his cart. Although the building line on the right hand side of the street is still recognisable today, the Kings Mall shopping centre, opened in 1979, now occupies the site opposite.

Traffic congestion in King Street at the junction with Hammersmith Grove in 1935. Parking space for delivery vehicles was restricted by the tram tracks that ran down the middle of the street. The new Marks & Spencer store on the left opened in 1932.

An unexpected and temporary view of St John the Evangelist Church, Glenthorne Road, from King Street, the result of a high-explosive bomb that fell on the night of 8 October 1940. The rubble from three shops is being conveyed away by lorry. King Street itself escaped relatively lightly from wartime bombing but other areas of the borough suffered heavier losses.

The Edwardian façade of the former Plough and Harrow Hotel, 122 King Street, has been preserved in the 2001 redevelopment. The building was the second hostelry of that name on the site and from 1960 was used as a showroom selling restored Rolls-Royce cars. It is intended that the old name will be preserved in a new licensed premises to be constructed on the King Street frontage.

Pleasant Place, a terrace of nine houses, was renumbered 312 to 328 Uxbridge Road in 1881. At that time three of the properties were occupied by people named Boarder, including Job Boarder, a builder, who employed 12 men and one apprentice. His house and business premises are shown at the end of the terrace, all of which has been demolished.

A patchwork of dilapidated buildings at the rear of 416 to 422 Uxbridge Road, lining the path leading to Bannister's Cottages. Hammersmith Council scheduled this area between Adelaide Road (now Grove) and Willow Vale to be cleared in the mid 1930s.

A more familiar scene in Uxbridge Road in the 1920s looking west from Frithville Gardens with the White Horse public house and the spire of St Stephen's Church on the left. Despite being a major thoroughfare there is plenty of space to park bicycles and a delivery cart against the pavement.

The Thames Water Ring Main Tower, incorporating a barometer, was the winning design in a competition for students of the Royal College of Art. Starting operation in 1994, it dominates the West Cross Route roundabout that straddles the borough boundary. This major road scheme obliterated the 19th-century landscape east of Shepherds Bush Green.

Protests about the dangers of traffic are not a modern phenomenon. The section of the Westway at the beginning of Western Avenue was a particular hazard, especially to children, three of whom had been killed in 1936 while crossing the road. In January 1937 concerned parents continued their campaign to obtain a 30mph speed limit.

Around Hammersmith Broadway

This chapter in particular looks at the area of Hammersmith around the Broadway, which has perhaps changed more than any other part of the borough since World War Two. Trends and developments that have altered and continue to alter the urban landscape can be seen here with particular clarity.

John Salter's map of Hammersmith in 1830 shows houses along King Street surrounded by gardens and orchards. The road layout would be unrecognisable today, with no roundabout at Hammersmith Broadway, no Butterwick, no Great West Road and very few of the streets that now run off King Street and the northern end of Fulham Palace Road yet built.

Hammersmith Creek, crossed by the High Bridge, was a working waterway with wharves and barges. Buildings then in existence such as the old workhouse on the site of Shortlands, Cromwell's Brewery in King Street and the Friends Meeting House near the Creek have since disappeared completely.

James Pollard's painting of the Broadway and Queen Street, dating from a few years after Salter's map, shows the first church of St Paul, Hammersmith, built in 1630-1, surrounded by old houses. Already, as the presence of a passenger coach, a public house and shops indicate, Hammersmith had grown beyond a village, thriving economically as a result of its position on one of the main routes out of London towards the west. Indeed the local historian Thomas Faulkner wrote in his *History and Antiquities of the Parish of Hammersmith* (1839) that '(Hammersmith) may be considered as a busy neighbourhood, and as one of the greatest thoroughfares in England.' According to Faulkner the building of the first Hammersmith Bridge in 1827 stimulated local improvements, so that the area began to go up in the world. Gas lighting had also arrived following an Act of Parliament in 1821.

The next 80 years were a period of rapid progress, accelerated by new transport links. The population of Hammersmith rose from 5,600 people in 1801 to 24,519 in 1861 and increased to 112,233 in 1901. The Hammersmith and City Railway (now the Hammersmith and City Line) station in Hammersmith opened in 1864, and the Metropolitan District Railway (now the District Line) station in 1874. Bradmore House was bought by the London General Omnibus Company Ltd in 1913 and converted into a garage for the petrol-driven buses that were taking over from horse buses. To cope with the increasing traffic, the Broadway was widened at the junction with Brook Green Road (now Shepherds Bush Road) in the early years of the 20th century. A network of residential streets was built around King Street and Queen Street (now Queen Caroline Street), while larger shops began to be erected, such as Palmers Stores, which stood where Blacks Road joins Queen Caroline Street. Old St Paul's was demolished and replaced by a much larger church in 1882. The Vestry Hall was opened in 1897 in Brook Green Road (now Shepherds Bush Road) and was not pulled down until 1962, although replaced in 1939 by the present Hammersmith Town Hall in King Street. Two major arrivals in Hammersmith Road were the West London Hospital, opened in 1856, and St. Paul's School, which moved in 1884 from the city into a large range of buildings designed by Alfred Waterhouse, now mostly demolished. New theatres, including the Palace of Varieties and the Lyric in King Street, and the King's Theatre in Hammersmith Road, catered for the leisure needs of the growing population. In 1936 Hammersmith Creek was filled in, and after the war Furnival Gardens were landscaped where previously there had been industrial activity and poor housing in an area known as Little Wapping.

The Broadway area escaped major bomb damage during World War Two, but a period of large-scale road building and redevelopment began soon after and altered the locality more effectively than any air raids. Butterwick was constructed in the late 1950s and the bus station was sited there until the 1990s, when a new bus station was incorporated in the Broadway Shopping Centre redevelopment. On 16 November 1961 the flyover that carries the A4 west out of London was opened. Buildings such as St Paul's Church of England School, the Britannia and the Six Bells public houses were demolished to make way for it, as well as several streets of houses between the underground railway line and Talgarth Road. Fuller's confectionery factory in Talgarth Road closed soon afterwards and was replaced by the Cunard International Hotel, since renamed the Novotel. In 1966 Hammersmith Power Station in Fulham Palace Road closed and was pulled down immediately. The first tall commercial building in Hammersmith was Hammersmith House, Hammersmith Bridge Road, erected in 1961 and now occupied by United Distillers. The Bredero Centre West development in the middle of the Broadway roundabout was preceded by many years of debate and alternative designs, finally getting under way in the late 1980s.

New building has continued apace in Hammersmith. In 1992 the Ark was opened on the site of a police car pound opposite the Novotel in Talgarth Road, followed soon after by the new West London Magistrates Court on its east side and the British Transport Police Station to the west. The Bredero Centre West development has also been extended. The Hammersmith Surgery building designed by Guy Greenfield and built in 2000, tucked in behind the flyover in Hammersmith Bridge Road, has been highly praised by architectural writers.

Many of the prestigious office buildings of Hammersmith are now tenanted by international companies such as Walt Disney, Coca-Cola, Polygram, United International Pictures and L'Oreal. No doubt they are attracted to the area by cheaper rents than central London and ease of access to Heathrow following the extension of the Piccadilly Line to the airport in 1977.

A view of St Paul's Church and Queen Street (now Queen Caroline Street) from the Broadway, painted around 1835 by James Pollard. Behind the carriage the sign entices travellers over the recently erected bridge by the promise of 'tolls much lower than other bridges'. By the early 19th century Hammersmith was a major transport centre for coach routes to and from London.

The drinking fountain provides an island for pedestrians negotiating the traffic in the Broadway around 1900. The tower of Hammersmith Town Hall in Brook Green Road (now Shepherds Bush Road) is prominent in this photograph taken from the corner of King Street.

In 1911 the north side of the Broadway was widened to cope with the increasing traffic. Among the property demolished was the 17th-century The George public house, formerly known as the White Horse. A new building, also named The George, was constructed on the yard and stables to the rear and opened on 19 August 1911, the day after the old hostelry closed its doors forever.

The road widening scheme of 1911 and a later one of 1923 swept away all the buildings on the corner of the Broadway and Brook Green Road (Shepherds Bush Road), shown here in 1908. The fire station next to the Broadway Congregational Church was rebuilt in 1913. Broadway Chambers, constructed in 1924, now occupies this corner site.

The Bon Marché, photographed in 1903, was one of Hammersmith's early department stores. It was situated in Bridge Terrace, at the western corner of the Broadway at its junction with Bridge Road (later Hammersmith Bridge Road). During World War One the adjoining family business of Palmers expanded to occupy most of the site.

The tower of the new church of St Paul was completed in 1889 and can be seen clearly in this drawing of 1900. The leisurely pace of pedestrians strolling in the roadway can be ascribed to artistic licence as eight years later the Broadway was described as 'an inferno owing to the heavy motor traffic, especially omnibuses, and to elderly people quite as dangerous as a field of battle'.

Shops at the Broadway entrance to Hammersmith District Line Station about 1913. The original station, built in 1874, was destroyed by fire in 1882 and rebuilt the same year. During the latest redevelopment of the station in the 1990s, some of the ceramic tiles that can be seen on the frontage were used as decorative features on internal walls.

A traffic jam in the Broadway in 1932. Trams and buses jostle for position with cars and delivery vans under the direction of a lone traffic policeman. Hammersmith Broadway did not become part of a one-way system until the late 1950s when a new road, Butterwick, was opened.

The disappearance of trams as a form of public transport eased traffic congestion at major road junctions. By the early 1950s drivers did not have to contend with tram tracks in the Broadway but the turn into King Street was still precarious. Pedestrians had the assistance of zebra crossings.

This photograph of Queen Caroline Street and the Broadway area was taken from the tower of St Paul's Church in April 1954. In the right foreground is the London Transport bus garage with an entrance through the Bradmore House façade. On the opposite side of Queen Caroline Street the Broadway Cinema is showing *The Weak and the Wicked* starring Glynis Johns.

This photograph, taken from a similar angle in 2001, shows how the area has changed almost beyond recognition. In Hammersmith Road the former West London Hospital and the neighbouring building, formerly the Royal London Mutual Insurance Society, can be identified. The only surviving building in Queen Caroline Street is the frontage of Bradmore House.

Hammersmith House, then the headquarters of The British Oxygen Company, can be seen through the rain beyond the Broadway Cinema at the junction of Queen Caroline Street and Hammersmith Bridge Road in 1965. The cinema opened in 1913 and closed in September 1977 following the collapse of the ceiling. It was demolished the following year.

Bradmore House was built in the early 18th century as an extension to Butterwick House and later became a separate residence. In 1913 it was bought by the London General Omnibus Company to convert into a garage. Before the house was demolished the company preserved some of the fittings and took down the east-facing garden façade to re-erect as the front elevation. This formed the Queen Caroline Street entrance to the bus garage, shown top in 1985. The retention and restoration of this historic façade was a key element in the redevelopment of the Broadway Centre. Work in progress in May 1990, bottom, shows the façade in isolation before reconstruction began. The building is now a restaurant.

Previous page and above: Forty years separates these views of the western section of the Hammersmith Flyover. The scale of the construction and its effect upon central Hammersmith cannot be underestimated. The flyover passes close to St Paul's Primary School, Worlidge Street, clearly shown on the left in 1961. Partly obscuring the school buildings in 2001 is the tower block of the London headquarters of the multinational company Universal Music. The striking white jagged roofline of the Hammersmith Surgery now occupies the waste site fronting Hammersmith Bridge Road.

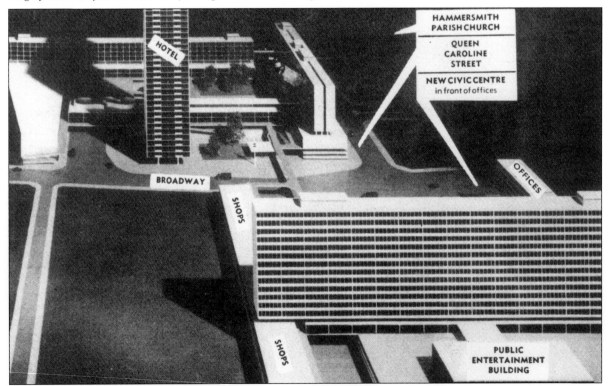

Between 1960 and 1988 several schemes were proposed for the redevelopment of the 14-acre Hammersmith Broadway site. This example from 1960 was rejected. A radical design in 1985 by the architect Norman Foster, consisting of a translucent plastic bubble enclosing a central area the size of Trafalgar Square, was equally unsuccessful.

Looking east from Hammersmith House on Hammersmith Bridge Road considerable changes are evident in little more than a decade. In 1960 the piers supporting the flyover are in place beside St Paul's Church. Beyond the church tower the Empress State Building in Lillie Road is under construction. The three chimneys to the right of the tower mark the site of Hammersmith Power station, behind the Guinness Trust Buildings in Fulham Palace Road. By 1973 multi-storeyed office blocks and the recently built Cunard International Hotel dominate the Broadway area. To the right the newly opened Charing Cross Hospital rises above the surrounding streets. (1960 photograph reproduced by kind permission of London Metropolitan Archives.)

The impact of the Hammersmith Flyover can be seen in the eight years separating these two photographs. Looking east from the tower of St Paul's Church in April 1954 the narrow Great Church Lane is lined with buildings. Rednall Terrace stretches away to the right behind the railway line and the Guinness Trust Buildings. By 1962 the construction of the Cromwell Road extension (Talgarth Road) had resulted in the demolition of a large section of the southern side of Great Church Lane including the Britannia public house and surrounding properties on the junction of Fulham Palace Road. Vehicles were able to make a right-hand turn from the recently opened Butterwick into the one-way traffic system.

In 2001 the view from the church tower is dominated by the buildings of the 1990s Broadway development of offices and shops. The striking design of The Ark occupies the curved site alongside the railway line formerly covered by Rednall Terrace. Amidst the modern architecture part of the reconstructed 18th-century Bradmore House can be seen in the left foreground.

Isolated on a strip of land at the corner of Queen Caroline Street in 1955, the Six Bells public house was demolished four years later for the construction of the flyover. Originally a terrace of houses and shops occupied the site. Behind the pub stands the Gaumont, opened in 1932, later renamed the Odeon Cinema and now known as the London Apollo.

A view southward across the roof of the London Apollo in 2001 shows the extent of the development at the northern end of Fulham Palace Road. North of Charing Cross Hospital is the extensive office block of a major publishing company next to the Guinness Trust Buildings. St Augustine's Roman Catholic Church, hall and presbytery separates these from the curved roof of the British Transport Police headquarters.

Hammersmith Bus and Coach Station, Butterwick, in 1979. The rudimentary facilities offered to waiting passengers contrast greatly with those now available within the Broadway Centre. Butterwick, named after the 16th-century house that stood in the vicinity, was constructed in the late 1950s.

The westward approach to the Hammersmith Flyover is very different in these photographs from 1961 and 1978. Fuller's confectionery factory was sold in 1964 and subsequently the 664-room Cunard International Hotel was built on the site. The hotel incorporated an air terminal, reflecting the fact that Hammersmith had direct road and rail links to Heathrow Airport via the Great West Road, the M4 and the Piccadilly Line. The French company Novotel bought the hotel in 1983. The earlier photograph shows electrical work in progress on the flyover. The installation of heating cables prevented ice forming on the roadway.

Two pictures showing Central Hammersmith in 2001. Moving eastwards from the glazed United Distillers office block, the extensive Ashcroft Square housing complex in King Street is clearly visible. This and the Lyric Theatre, seen at the left of the lower photograph, forms part of the King's Mall development. Commercial offices and the Irish Centre have been built on the triangular site that was formerly the Broadway Cinema. To the right of the Citibank offices, Hammersmith Grove is clearly delineated by its avenue of trees. In the foreground part of the recently landscaped St Paul's Green separates the church from Hammersmith Bridge Road.

Lyric Square from the balcony of the Lyric Theatre in September 2001. The pedestrianised southern end of Hammersmith Grove is a public space between King Street and Beadon Road. In the foreground are the striped awnings of the stalls in the long-established Hammersmith market, started over a century ago in King Street. Improvements to Lyric Square are planned for the future.

Beadon Road has changed greatly in nature and appearance within the last 30 years. Late 19th century terraces of shops and small businesses serving the vicinity preceded the construction of the Citibank and United International Pictures offices on the west side of the street shown here in 2001.

Shops and Markets

Until the 19th century such shops as existed in Hammersmith and Fulham catered for a very local clientele. Fresh fruit and vegetables were available from the market gardens in the area and local farms and cow keepers provided dairy products. Gradually, as prosperous houses were built along the river in Hammersmith or down Fulham High Street, shops began to appear that sold goods such as clothes and household necessities to the carriage trade. Vendors also sold items from baskets that they carried around with them from house to house or placed on the pavement, and handcarts and small horse-drawn vehicles were used to take goods to customers.

By the early years of the 20th century, building development and the growing population had attracted many small shops to the streets and terraces of Hammersmith and Fulham, as well as some larger drapers' establishments. The era of the department store was also beginning. Walham Green in Fulham and King Street in Hammersmith were the main shopping centres, and shop opening hours were long, often until 11.00pm in the week and even later on Saturdays. Goods were displayed in profusion outside shops, including perishable foodstuffs, and small dairy farms such as Glover's Dairy at 15 Brook Green Road, and Vicarage Dairy Farm at 796 Fulham Road, still provided fresh milk and dairy products. Milk was ladled from the churn on floats and other goods were sold on the streets in barrows, drawn by a pony or perhaps a bicycle.

The larger establishments included Barbers and Timothy Davies in Fulham and Palmers in Hammersmith. Timothy Davies, who was Mayor of Fulham and later its MP in the first decade of the 20th century, opened his draper's shop at Fulham Broadway in 1885. By the 1930s the shop had grown into a department store occupying 30,000 sq ft, but it was sold during World War Two. F.H. Barber, who founded Barbers in North End Road, also became Mayor of Fulham. His shop, which opened in 1891, eventually occupied a whole block and was open until the 1990s. Palmers stood where Blacks Road now joins Queen Caroline Street, on the site of an earlier shop called Bon Marché. Until it closed in 1953 it sold food, clothing, household furnishings and china and glass. Road junctions sometimes took their names from well-known shops, such as Poppy's Corner at the junction of Lillie Road and North End Road, named after A.W. Poppy's ladies' outfitters store, which existed there between about 1900 and 1924.

Shops and other commercial premises reflect changing tastes and fashions. In the late 19th century eating establishments were often called dining rooms and catered mainly for men, serving chops and other meat dishes. By the 1920s teashops, such as those provided by J. Lyons and Co., were becoming popular, especially with women who were increasingly joining the workforce and needed somewhere to have lunch on a working day or while shopping. After the war Italian ice-cream parlours and trattorias enjoyed a craze, but they, in their turn, have been replaced by coffee-shop chains, bars and a wide variety of restaurants.

The borough has some long-established markets. North End Road Market is thought to have started in the 1880s when costers moved there from the western end of Kings Road. Although the stalls tend to restrict traffic in the road, the market shows no signs of dying. Hammersmith Market, which is at least a century old and sold mainly fruit, vegetables, fish and flowers, survives in a very limited form. It moved into Bradmore Lane in 1906 and then into Hammersmith Grove in the 1970s. Shepherds Bush Market was opened in 1914 in what had formerly been the access road to the old Shepherds Bush Metropolitan Line Station, replaced in the same year by two new stations in Goldhawk Road and Uxbridge Road. There were already shops in the railway arches, and the shopkeepers were unhappy when costers were allowed to set up their barrows in competition, objecting also to the noise and the smell of fish from the fish stalls. Their protests were unsuccessful and although Shepherds Bush Market closed during World War One and was bombed during World War Two, it survived and still flourishes.

In the decades since World War Two the pattern of shopping has changed. The effects of wartime bombing and changes in working practices meant that small shops were not in a good position to fend off competition from the new supermarkets that opened from the 1950s onwards. One of the earliest in the area was the Lyons supermarket in Hammersmith Road, opened in February 1956 and at that time the largest in West London. In 1979 the King's Mall shopping centre opened in King Street, incorporating the rebuilt Lyric Theatre. The Hammersmith Broadway Shopping Centre was part of the Bredero Centre West redevelopment of Hammersmith tube and bus stations in the early 1990s. Supermarkets have been built on land vacated by departing industries, including a Sainsburys store on the former Fulham Power Station site at Sands End and a branch of Tesco on the Osram Works site at Brook Green. Chain stores have tended to replace the local drapers' shops, chemists, shoe shops, opticians, stationers and similar businesses. In Fulham, many antique, furniture and interior decoration outlets have opened to cater for the affluent people who are buying homes in the area. In the near future there will be major retail opportunities at Fulham Broadway, where the underground station complex is being redeveloped, and at Wood Lane where a large shopping centre is planned.

For most of the 19th century the Mundy family dealt in glass, china and earthenware at their shop on the south side of Hammersmith Broadway. The last owner was Miss Sarah Frances Mundy. The shop, along with a linen drapers and a stationers, was demolished in about 1879. The fine fan detail over the door suggests that the building dated from the early 18th century.

Hanes & Co. sold pianos and musical instruments at this address on the corner of Darlan Road between 1902 and 1911, taking over from an earlier piano dealership. The piano was a familiar item in the Victorian and Edwardian home and could be bought on easy monthly terms. During World War One 578 Fulham Road became the home of the Central Hall Mission which remained there until 1925.

George Wombwell, his wife and daughter stand outside the Brook Green Dining Rooms, 166 Shepherds Bush Road in about 1908. A notice in the window advertises the Men's League Sick Benefit Society: possibly this was an agency office. In 2002 the premises is still a restaurant although a menu including sun-dried tomatoes and goat's cheese would be unlikely in 1908. (Reproduced by kind permission of Mr G. Wombwell.)

A long standing name in King Street was Messrs Leonard E. Jolly Ltd, established on the corner of Bradmore Lane for almost half a century. This photograph of 1911 was taken to display the Christmas stock of poultry and hams as well as the usual cooked meat and tinned provisions. The shop eventually expanded from the cramped premises of 24d King Street into the adjoining property.

The Holton family was a well established name in the butchers' trade in the 19th and early 20th centuries. Both properties shown here were butchers' shops in King Street by 1860, although Thomas Holton only took over 158 King Street in the late 1880s. His name can be seen in the tiles underneath the left-hand window in the photograph of about 1890. By 1901 Thomas Holton no longer lived on the premises and the business had expanded to include the adjoining four properties. There was a Benjamin Holton, butcher, at 49 King Street in 1860. Fifty years later staff pose in front of the carcasses, joints and tongues exposed to the King Street traffic.

In 1911 prospective house buyers could find their needs met at Gale's Corner on the junction of Fulham Road with Jerdan Place. George A. Gale was an estate developer, Binns & Douglas were estate agents and auctioneers, and J. Macdonald & Co. were builders. The spread of urban development continued into the surrounding areas as testified by the placard advertising ideal homes in East Sheen.

Arthur Batho, grocer, oilman, sugar retailer and general store keeper was established at 30 Caxton Road, Shepherds Bush, by 1919 and was trading at that address until at least 1941. His delivery van is a reminder that motor vehicles had not completely superseded the horse in the years following World War One.

Hairdresser. **E. CROSS.** Tobacconist.

HAIR CUTTING. SHAMPOOING.

TADDY'S IMPERIAL TOBACCO

PARK DRIVE

MURATTIS HIGH CLASS CIGARETTES

RAJAH

LAMBERT & BUTLER'S WAVERLEY CIGARETTES

LAMBERT & BUTLER'S WAVERLEY CIGARETTES 3/10

LEMAX SAFETY RAZOR

HAIR CUTTING & SHAVING

WAVERLEY CIGARETTES

MARCELLA 10 MARCELLA

WAVERLEY CIGARETTES

SHAVING

UMBRELLAS RE COVERED & REPAIRED

'Walk In Please. Walk Out Pleased' reads one of the hand-written notices on the window of this well-stocked hairdresser and tobacconist's shop at 768 Fulham Road. Edwin Cross traded here between 1916 and 1925. He also repaired umbrellas, one of which is hanging over the entrance.

SHAMPOOING 4ᴰ   SHAVING 2ᴰ   HAIR CUTTING 4ᴰ

The Fulham Drug Company's registered office had a brief existence at 351 Lillie Road between 1925 and 1928. The property was formerly the drug store of Mrs Marie Thompson and was later occupied by Leonard Sanderson, chemist. A variety of patent medicines and tonics could be purchased and a weighing machine outside the shop was available to customers.

There were a number of ice-cream vendors of Italian origin living in the borough in the early years of the 20th century. By 1901 three Italian families had made their home at 1 Everington Street, Fulham. Achille Santilli, of that address, seen here about 1922, sold ice cream from a handcart around the streets.

A hairdressing establishment was at 635 Fulham Road from the time of World War One. Harry Dersh took over the business in 1923 and remained there until 1955. This view of the interior of the shop in the early 1930s was possibly taken for publicity purposes for Jarvis and Co. of London who were suppliers of hairdressing equipment and sundries.

Charles Baker and Co. Ltd of High Holborn opened a new branch of their gentlemen's and boys' clothing store at 31-33 King Street, Hammersmith, in September 1896, expanding to numbers 27 and 29 two years later. This photograph was taken about 1930 before the building was purchased by Marks & Spencer who built a new shop on the site in 1932. (Reproduced by kind permission of Marks & Spencer Company Archives.)

Lyons' Staff Stores opened at Cadby Hall, Hammersmith Road in 1915. Although at first the shop was intended to serve Lyons' workforce it was later opened to the public. It retained the original name until 1956 when it was converted into Lyons Supermarket. Rationing was still in force in 1949 when this photograph was taken. The customer at the head of the queue is paying for her bacon with coupons.

In addition to being a food manufacturer, the firm of J. Lyons & Co. was a commercial caterer and ran the famous national chain of teashops. Counter staff were trained in the art of window dressing as demonstrated by this display in the Hammersmith Broadway teashop in 1951.

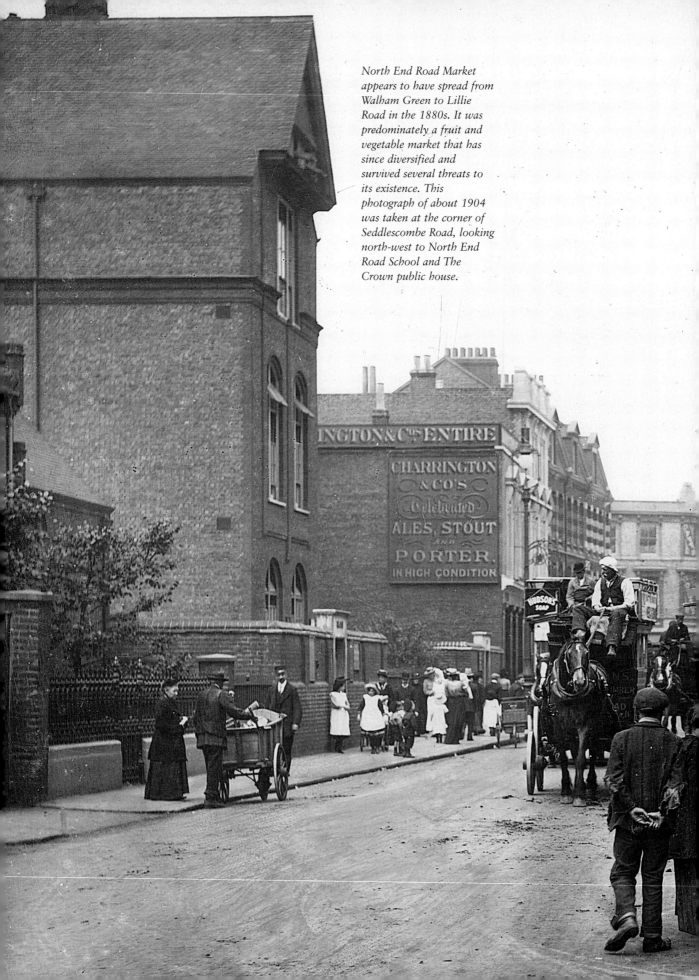

North End Road Market appears to have spread from Walham Green to Lillie Road in the 1880s. It was predominately a fruit and vegetable market that has since diversified and survived several threats to its existence. This photograph of about 1904 was taken at the corner of Seddlescombe Road, looking north-west to North End Road School and The Crown public house.

Scalas Ice Cream Parlour, 387 North End Road, in 1955. After bomb damage during World War Two, the cafeteria was rebuilt in a modern style incorporating the best hygiene practices, such as easily cleaned surfaces and a steam canopy extractor. Neon lights and mirror tiles complemented the glass and stainless steel counter. There was also an ice-cream kiosk at the front of the shop, facing the market. (Reproduced by kind permission of the Public Record Office.)

Although the official opening of Shepherds Bush Market was on 3 July 1914, its origins go back to the previous century when the railway arches on the approach road to the first Shepherds Bush station were converted into shops. When the station was closed in 1914 the railway company granted licences to sublet pitches and the roadway was paved. The market expanded rapidly after World War One and extensions were opened in 1929 and 1932; in 1938 an entrance from Uxbridge Road was added. Shepherds Bush has remained a large and popular market with permanent and temporary stalls selling a wide range of goods. Two scenes from 1953 show the variety on offer from women's clothing to packets of joss sticks.

Notable Houses

The borough used to have a number of fine houses that were built by wealthy men who found the area attractive because it was rural enough to offer space and healthy air, yet not many miles from London. Later these houses were demolished when Hammersmith and Fulham became built up and therefore less exclusive. In a few cases they survive, despite being threatened by modern development all around, and sometimes the grounds were saved and turned into public parks.

Some houses did not last into the age of photography. Queen Catherine of Braganza (1638-1705), wife of Charles II, lived intermittently in a house in Hammersmith on the site of Rivercourt Road where it meets Upper Mall. The house had large grounds and an orangery, and in 1702 a newspaper advertisement offered a reward for the recovery of 69 striped hollies and other shrubs stolen from her garden. Brandenburgh House, on the river west of Hammersmith Bridge, was built by Sir Nicholas Crisp (c.1599–1669), a wealthy slave trader who supported Charles I during the Civil War. In the early 19th century Caroline of Brunswick, George IV's ill-fated Queen, came to live at Brandenburgh House and she died there soon after being turned away from his coronation in 1821. The house was demolished and the site redeveloped to become Hammersmith Distillery.

Many of the borough's large houses were pulled down in the late 19th century when pressure for building land increased, but others survived longer, some to within living memory. Broom House, in Broomhouse Lane, was a large, elegant 18th-century house on the river east of Hurlingham House. The Sulivan family took over the house in 1823; the Prime Minister Lord Palmerston used to visit Laurence Sulivan, who was a government minister, and it was said that the plan for the Crimean War was virtually arranged on the lawn there. The house was demolished after the death in 1911 of Miss Sulivan, who was a local benefactor and made many charitable gifts of land. Ravenscourt Park House in Hammersmith was Georgian, built on the foundations of the earlier Pallingswick manor house. In 1888 the grounds became a public park and the house was used as a public library until it was destroyed by a bomb in 1941. The Grange, North End, home of both the novelist Samuel Richardson and the artist Edward Burne-Jones, was built as a double house in the second decade of the 18th century. It was demolished in 1957 after an unsuccessful campaign to save it, and a local authority housing block was built on the site.

The most important of the few grand houses that still survive is Fulham Palace, the former country residence for a thousand years of the Bishops of London, who were also Lords of the Manor of Fulham. The existing palace dates from different periods, and was formerly surrounded by a moat and extensive gardens that were well stocked by several of the bishops who were expert horticulturists. The grounds became a public park in 1893 and part of the palace now houses a museum. Kelmscott House on the river at Upper Mall, Hammersmith, built in the late 1780s, is in private occupancy and the lower floor is tenanted by the William Morris Society. Kelmscott House was the home of Morris, a designer, poet and socialist, between 1878 and 1896, and Morris furnished the house throughout with his own fabrics and furniture designed by friends such as Philip Webb. Kelmscott House is surrounded by other old properties, for example nearby Sussex House, a handsome building dating from around 1726. Hurlingham House on the river at Fulham, completed in 1803 but incorporating part of an earlier house of 1760, still stands in splendid isolation in its extensive grounds.

Other houses have not been so fortunate. Modern buildings tower over Bradmore House, in Queen Caroline Street, now a restaurant but for many years before that a bus garage. Bradmore House, which was originally an extension of an old house called Butterwick House, dates from the early 18th century and has been so extensively rebuilt that only the façade remains. Sandford Manor, in Rewell Street, was built in the 17th century and soon began to be used for industrial purposes as a saltpetre factory, a cloth factory, then a caskmaking establishment and finally a bleach and dye works, until the estate was bought in 1823 by the Imperial Gas Company and Fulham Gasworks was established on the site. The house became part of the gasworks complex and was extensively restored in the 1980s.

The restoration work at Fulham House, near Putney Bridge in Fulham High Street, which dates originally from the early 18th century, has involved pulling down some unsightly accretions to the house, revealing its original dignified appearance. At one time it was planned to demolish the house, but campaigners were able to save it.

In addition to the grand houses of the borough there were many comfortable houses built in the late 18th and 19th centuries that were large by today's standards, accommodating big families and several servants. Some of these houses became private schools, for example Kent House at 10 Lower Mall, which still stands. Built in c.1762 in the Adam style, it housed a boys' school in the 19th century that is said to have numbered Sir Thomas Stamford Raffles (1781–1826), colonial governor and Far Eastern expert, among its pupils. Other houses were used as private lunatic asylums, of which there were a number in Fulham in Victorian times. Normand House, which stood north of Lillie Road, was a 17th-century house that was later used successively as an asylum for insane ladies, a school and then as a refuge for female ex-prisoners run by the nuns of the St Katherine's Sisterhood. Normand House was destroyed by a bomb during World War Two.

Broom House was an imposing house overlooking the river west of Broomhouse Road (now Lane). This photograph was taken in 1910, a year before its demolition. The Sulivan family owned the house between 1823 and 1911 and its last occupier was Miss Charlotte Sulivan, who sold to the council the freehold of Southfields, on which South Park was formed. The grounds of Broom House now form part of Hurlingham Club.

East End House, seen here in a drawing published in 1860, was situated on the south-east corner of Parsons Green, surrounded by 16 acres of grounds. It was originally an Elizabethan property called Hollybush House, but was remodelled and renamed in the late 18th century. Its occupiers included Mrs. Fitzherbert, the morganatic wife of the Prince Regent (later George IV). The house was demolished in 1884.

Between 1728 and 1853 this building in Back Lane (now Burlington Road) was used as a boarding school known first as Fulham Academy and later as Burlington House School. The house and grounds were then bought by the government as the site of the Fulham Refuge, later Fulham Women's Convict Prison. The house was retained as officers' quarters and was demolished in 1895, seven years after the prison closed.

The tower of All Saints, Fulham, can be seen behind Thames Bank, which stood close to the river on the west side of Putney Bridge. The house, which had gardens running down to the water, was probably built around 1800 and was described in 1841 as 'a neat stuccoed cottage residence'. It was demolished in about 1895 and the site was added to Bishops Park.

The Grange, 38-40 North End Crescent, photographed shortly before demolition in 1957. The house was built around 1714 and was actually two houses incorporated into a single building. The novelist Samuel Richardson lived at the Grange in the mid 18th century, and between 1867 and 1898 it was the home of the artist Sir Edward Burne-Jones, who had a studio in the garden.

Holy Cross House in Fulham Road stands behind hoardings in 1896, two years before it was demolished to make way for shops. Among the posters are advertisements for shows at Olympia. The house may have dated from the mid 18th century, and was used as a school in the early 19th century. From 1881 the Wantage Sisterhood ran a hospital for chronically-ill women and children in the house.

Cambridge House was situated immediately to the west of old Fulham Bridge, a pier of which can be seen in the foreground of this pre-1886 photograph. The house was built in 1843 on the site of the former stables of Fulham Hall. Cambridge House became the White Lodge Laundry, 156 High Street, in the early years of the 20th century, and last appeared in the Kelly's local directory in 1906/7.

New Kings Primary School, now stands on the site of Draycott Lodge in New Kings Road. The house was built around 1813 and the Pre-Raphaelite artist William Holman Hunt lived there between 1879 and 1902. Hunt had travelled and painted in the Middle East, and his taste for the art of that region can be seen in this 1893 photograph of the boudoir taken from the drawing room.

The Grange, Brook Green, was the home of the famous actor Sir Henry Irving between 1881 and 1889. Irving restored the house at great expense, but it proved to be too far from the West End theatres. This photograph may have been taken at about the time it was sold to the Governors of St Paul's School in 1895. St Paul's Girls' School was opened on the site in 1904.

Brook Green House, which stood near the present junction of Girdlers Road and Brook Green, was opened in 1760 as a school for girls at risk from vice. The school, which was rebuilt in 1787, evolved into a Roman Catholic boarding school for girls. In 1850 the building was taken over by St Mary's Roman Catholic teachers' training college, and it was demolished in 1903 when the college was expanded.

The conservatory at Wood House, an early 19th-century property which lay on the east side of Wood Lane above the present Bulwer Street. The house was noted for its grounds, and in 1894 they were opened to the public, with a full-size replica of Stonehenge and balloon ascents among the attractions. The venture failed, and soon after the estate was acquired by the Central London Railway Company Ltd.

Cromwell House, 207 King Street, was the residence of Joseph Cromwell, who founded the Cromwell Brewery in about 1780. The house and brewery were situated at the head of Hammersmith Creek, which was once navigable as far as King Street. The house was demolished to make way for the Blue Hall Cinema, opened in 1912.

The early 18th-century Ravenscourt Park House, seen here in an Edwardian postcard, stood on the site of an older moated house called Pallingswick Manor. In 1887 the Scott family sold the Ravenscourt Park estate to the Metropolitan Board of Works. The house became a public library, while the grounds were turned into a park. The library was damaged beyond repair by incendiary bombs in January 1941.

Marlesford Lodge, 241 King Street, was built in the 1860s. Around 1885 it became a school run by the Kensington & Chelsea Board of Guardians for workhouse children, some of whom can be seen in this photograph. By 1932 it had become a London County Council children's home, which closed after the war. The building is now called Palingswick House and is a centre for Community Organisations.

Part of the dining room of Kelmscott House, 26 Upper Mall, Hammersmith. The house was built in the late 18th century and between 1878 and 1896 was the London home of William Morris, who furnished it with his own fabrics and wallpapers. The photograph was taken at about the time he died in 1896. The house is now privately occupied and the lower floor houses the William Morris Society.

This undated photograph of the stables at Parkside, Ravenscourt Park, is a reminder of the ancillary buildings necessary for the smooth running of a large household. Built in the mid 19th century, the house became the Parkside Officers (Orthopaedic) Hospital in World War One. It was then used as a maternity home for a few years before being demolished to make way for the Royal Masonic Hospital, opened in 1933.

Sport and Entertainment

Public houses often have early origins, although they may have been altered or rebuilt over the centuries. A document dated 1722 is the first to list pubs in Hammersmith by name, and some of them are still in existence, for example Hogs, now the Hampshire Hog in King Street. During the 19th century many new pubs were built to serve the rapidly expanding population, and by 1873 there were 139 in Hammersmith alone. At the end of that century there was a trend towards smartening pubs by rebuilding and enlarging them, as happened for example at the Crabtree pub in 1898 when it was rebuilt with a billiards room and a function room. Today there are fewer pubs, and many have been renamed and altered inside to attract a younger clientele.

Three major exhibition centres, two of which remain, were located in the borough: White City, Earls Court and Olympia. The site of Earls Court, which is shared with the neighbouring Royal Borough of Kensington and Chelsea, was laid out on surplus railway land and the first exhibition was the America Exhibition of 1887, featuring Buffalo Bill's Wild West Show. Imre Kiralfy (1845–1919), the great Hungarian exhibitions' maestro, was Director General of Exhibitions at Earls Court from 1895 until 1914, mounting shows such as the Golden West Exhibition, the Balkan States Exhibition and the Military Exhibition. In the inter-war period the site was rebuilt as a more permanent exhibition centre, and Earls Court 2 was constructed on the Hammersmith and Fulham side of the boundary in 1989-91. The Grand Hall at Olympia, which covered an area of four acres, was opened in 1886 on land once occupied by Lee and Kennedy's nursery. The venue became famous for its circuses, including those of Barnum and Bailey and Bertram Mills. Imre Kiralfy produced spectacles at Olympia such as *Venice in London* in 1891, and the venue later hosted the Motor Show,

the International Horse Show, and the Daily Mail Ideal Home Exhibition. The National Hall and Empire Hall were added in 1923 and 1929.

The White City was built in 1907-8 on 140 acres of farmland in Shepherds Bush, and was named after a similar exhibition that had taken place in Chicago. It was built for the Franco-British Exhibition of 1908, created by Imre Kiralfy and consisting of some 20 palaces, 120 smaller buildings, water features and special amusements like the Mountain Scenic Railway and the Flip-Flap. Among the attractions were the Machinery Hall, the Women's Work Palace, the Indian Palace, the Palace of French Applied Art, and Ballymaclinton, a recreated Irish village. The Franco-British Exhibition ran from 14 May to 31 October 1908, and was attended by 8,400,000 people. Later exhibitions at the White City included the Japan-British Exhibition (1910), which featured Japanese villages and tea gardens, and the Latin-British Exhibition (1912). World War One brought the era of great exhibitions at White City to an end, although the British Industries Fairs, which were essentially trade fairs, were held in the elevated entrance halls during the 1920s and 30s. The London County Council built the White City Estate on part of the site in 1936, and the BBC Television Centre was erected on another 13 acres in Wood Lane in 1949. The Shepherds Bush Exhibition Ltd company was finally wound up in 1963, and a shopping and leisure complex is now planned for the land on the other side of Wood Lane where the entrance arch and halls stood.

The borough has been a good place for spectator sports for well over a century. The Stadium at the White City was built for the 1908 Olympics, at which Great Britain, the host nation, had the advantage of providing all the officials, a practice that did not continue. The Stadium later hosted greyhound racing, speedway, boxing, athletics, the strange sport of cheetah racing, International Horse Shows, World Cup soccer in 1966, and even Queens Park Rangers' home games. It closed in 1984 and was demolished soon afterwards. The University Boat Race, which covers a distance of about four miles from Putney Bridge to Mortlake, is usually decided on the crucial loop of the river from Hammersmith Bridge to Chiswick Eyot. However, the most popular spectator sport of the last 100 years has been football, and the borough has three professional clubs within its boundaries that have all grown from small beginnings. Fulham Football Club, founded in 1879 as a humble boys team at St Andrew's Church, took over the site of the ruined Craven Cottage in 1894, and soon afterwards turned professional. They were promoted to the First Division (then the top football division) in 1959 and are now (2002) in the Premiership. Another Premiership club, Chelsea, who play at Stamford Bridge, were founded in 1905 and have had considerable success, being League Champions in 1955, FA

Cup winners in 1970, 1997 and 2000 (they reached the Final again in 2002), and winners of the European Cup-winners Cup in 1971 and 1998. They won the League Cup in 1965 and 1998. Second Division Queens Park Rangers were founded in 1886 but did not find a permanent home at Loftus Road until 1917. They won the League Cup in 1967 and were promoted to the old First Division in 1968, 1973 and 1983.

There have always been plenty of opportunities to participate in sport in the borough, although some have been restricted to the more affluent. Rowing and sculling clubs such as the London Corinthian Sailing Club are still active on the river. Hurlingham Club, formerly famous as a polo ground, and Queen's Club, specialising in tennis, provide exclusive sporting opportunities for their members. In the early 20th century public baths were opened in Shorrolds Road, Fulham, and at Lime Grove, Hammersmith. They have been replaced by modern facilities offering more than just swimming and slipper baths.

The old Crabtree, photographed around 1895, was the last of Fulham's riverside inns. Probably dating from the 18th century, it was formerly known as The Three Jolly Gardeners. It was demolished in 1898 to make way for the larger Crabtree Hotel that offered modern facilities such as a billiards saloon and a function hall.

A public house named The Kings Head has stood in Fulham High Street since the late 17th century. The property shown here in about 1903 was the second building on the site, opposite the junction with Fulham Road. It gained wide press coverage in 1905 when the London County Council paid the huge sum of £64,000 to demolish and rebuild most of the premises as part of a road-widening scheme.

A drayman poses with customers outside the Eight Bells in Fulham High Street around 1880. The name is thought to commemorate the peal of bells placed in All Saints Church tower in 1729. The barge carrying them from the bell foundry sank in the Thames but the bells were recovered undamaged. Situated by Fulham Bridge the inn enjoyed much passing trade but this was lost when Putney Bridge opened in 1886.

The Cock Hotel at 360 North End Road became renowned as a sporting pub in the early years of the 20th century. The licensee, Edward Thomas Pimm, owned prize-winning bull terriers. One of these, Sam Lavender, is shown with three human sporting champions in 1909. The Cock Hotel was built in the mid 1890s and replaced an older Cock tavern on the same site.

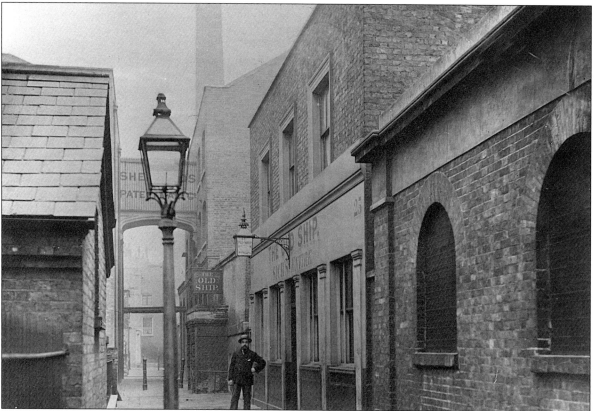

The entrance to the Old Ship, 25 Upper Mall, looking east towards Beavor Lane in the late 1890s. The remains of the old doorway to the original 17th-century Ship Inn can be seen beneath the hanging sign. The area was primarily industrial and the chimney of the nearby oil mills towers in the background. The Old Ship was also the headquarters of the Eyot Sailing Club.

The Red Cow and its rural surroundings in the 1860s. It was an 18th-century coaching inn situated on what is now the corner of Colet Gardens and Hammersmith Road. The old pub was replaced in 1897 by a larger building and, during the 1970s, became a well-known venue for live music. It has been renamed Latymers.

Cocktails were served in the American Bar at The Clarendon, shown here in the 1940s. This large hotel at 1, 3 & 5 Hammersmith Broadway offered many facilities, including a Masonic hall, banqueting suite, restaurants, bars and accommodation. The imposing frontage and the Art Deco interior made the hotel a local landmark. It was demolished in 1988 as part of the Broadway redevelopment scheme.

The ornate fittings and plush drapery of the saloon bar of the White Horse public house on the corner of Lime Grove and Uxbridge Road in 1910. The large building accommodated several bars that were removed during extensive alterations in 1970 when the interior was transformed into one huge bar room with a music area.

An inn has stood at the eastern end of Uxbridge Road at Shepherds Bush for over 160 years. Historically this was the main coaching route from London to Oxford and places west and this was reflected in the name of the pub. In 1908 the main entrance to the White City exhibition site was built next to the Mail Coach and the decorated arch is visible to the left of the old building. Completely rebuilt in the early 1930s, The Mail Coach now stands on the corner of the West Cross Route roundabout. The long structures of the White City exhibition halls can be seen clearly behind the arch in the photograph from 1973. This area is scheduled for considerable redevelopment.

Lillie Bridge Athletic Ground, opened in 1869, was laid out on land adjoining the railway line south of West Brompton Station. The ground was at the height of its success in the 1870s when it staged a variety of athletic events. A riot by dissatisfied spectators in 1887 hastened its decline and the site became a railway goods depot and is now a car park for the Earls Court Exhibition Halls.

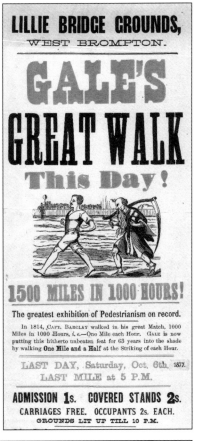

Adjacent to Lillie Bridge was another sporting venue at Beaufort House on the east side of North End Road, now covered by Seddlescombe Road. The extensive grounds had a rifle range and later became the headquarters of the South Middlesex Rifle Volunteers. Teams of Native Americans demonstrate the game of lacrosse in 1867.

Fulham Football Club began in 1879 as Fulham St Andrews, a church side founded by a Sunday school teacher at St Andrew's Church, Fulham Fields. In 1894 the club bought their permanent ground at Craven Cottage and played their first match there two years later. At the time of this photograph in 1903 the club had become a limited company and began to sign professional players.

Hammersmith Cricket Club probably began as a casual team in the 1870s. By the time of this 1890 tour of Norfolk the club had officially been in existence for 10 seasons. The club's ground was located near the junction of Du Cane Road and Wood Lane.

The White City Stadium was built for the 1908 Olympic Games. Some events did not attract many spectators as shown by the empty stands in this photograph. Despite breaking the Olympic record, E.B. Archibald of Canada was one of three athletes who tied for a bronze medal in the pole vault, with a height of 11 feet 9 inches.

In June 1927 the White City Stadium hosted the first London greyhound race meeting. Greyhound racing remained at the stadium until the last meeting held on 22 September 1984. The track, which was run by the Greyhound Racing Association, had the first photo-finish camera and the largest Tote in Britain. Workmen are shown here adjusting the adding machines in the Tote control room before the 1939 Greyhound Derby.

After 1908 the White City Stadium was the venue for a wide variety of sporting and other events and was the home of the annual International Horse Show for 20 years. This photograph shows a parade of competitors in 1958. The stadium was demolished in 1985 and the site is now part of the BBC headquarters in Wood Lane.

Chelsea Football Club was formed in 1905 at Stamford Bridge, a former athletics ground. During the course of the 20th century the site was improved and extended, culminating in the Chelsea Village development of the 1990s. Seen here from Fulham Road in 2001, the Village incorporates two hotels, restaurants, a private sports club and apartments.

Fulham Baths at Walham Green and Lime Grove Baths in Shepherds Bush were both constructed in the first decade of the 20th century and included public washhouses. Each site operated first and second class pools and initially mixed bathing was not permitted although, by 1920, it had been introduced at Lime Grove. The men's second-class pool at Fulham is shown in an undated photograph (top). Children enjoy the facilities of the former first-class pool at Lime Grove in 1978 (bottom). Both baths were closed by early 1981 and the Lime Grove site was redeveloped for housing. A dance studio now occupies the Fulham building in North End Road.

The 300ft-high steam-driven great wheel at Earls Court came into operation on 5 July 1895, and made an average of 30 journeys every day. It could carry up to 1,200 passengers in 40 cars, of which 10 were first-class. In 1906 the wheel stopped for 15 hours and 74 people were trapped overnight. The wheel closed in 1906 and was dismantled early the following year.

Indra the sacred elephant was exhibited at the 1908 Hungarian Exhibition at Earls Court as part of The Bostock Arena and Jungle, which featured 'Arenic Performances with Savage Beasts, Lions, Tigers, Bears, Leopards, Elephants etc.' Apart from other attractions such as the Ice Caverns, the exhibition concentrated on the arts, products and industries of Hungary. It was visited by 1,294,000 people.

The first permanent Earls Court Exhibition Centre hall was built in 1936-7 on the eastern part of the original site, outside the borough boundaries. A new hall, Earls Court 2, designed by RMJM, is shown here under construction in April 1990. Spanning the railway with a roof supported on 84-metre trusses, Earls Court 2 extends into Hammersmith and Fulham. Behind it stands the distinctive Empress State Building.

Two of the many postcards produced at the time of the Earls Court exhibitions, souvenirs of the attractions of the site. The steam-driven Flying Machine, which was a feature of several early 20th-century exhibitions there, was also known as Sir Hiram Maxim's Airship. Hiram Maxim, American by birth, was an inventor and engineer whose other inventions included the Maxim automatic gun. The Katzenjammer Castle, part of the 1909 Golden West and American Industries Exhibition, was a haunted castle as its appearance suggests. It was advertised as 'a weird novelty, full of mystery and amusement'. Other spectacles at The Golden West Exhibition included the Black Hawk Massacre, The Deluge and The Destruction of San Francisco.

Hopi Indians from the Painted Desert, Arizona, performed the sacred snake dance at the Mammoth Fun City show at Olympia in 1906. While the Fun City consisted of various shows and entertainments, the Royal Naval and Military Tournament of the same year displayed the prowess of the armed forces. It included a competition to see which mounted swordsman could excel in cutting lemons while riding at full speed.

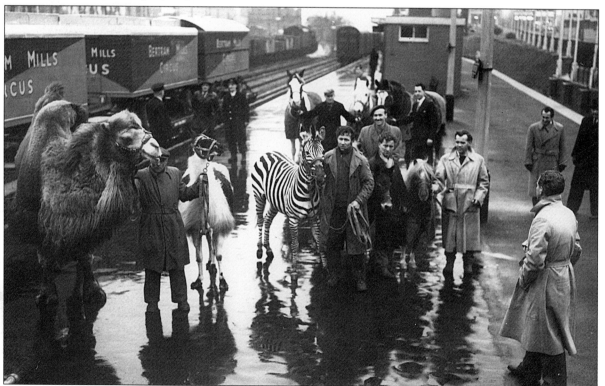

Although Olympia is now mainly used for commercial trade fairs, the large exhibition halls are suitable venues for spectaculars such as military displays and circuses. In the early years Barnum and Bailey's Circus performed at Olympia, and between 1920 and 1965 Bertram Mills' Circus was an annual fixture. Animals are seen arriving here with their handlers at Addison Road Station (now Kensington Olympia Station) for the 1957 season.

The buildings of the White City exhibition site were constructed of steel frames and concrete, covered by plaster mouldings painted white. The cascade in the central Court of Honour at the White City was one of several water features. Visitors could enjoy boat trips around the lagoons and canals for 6d. At night the cascade was illuminated by coloured lights and the surrounding buildings were outlined with white light bulbs.

The nocturnal appearance of the White City can be seen in this photograph of the Imperial Pavilion at the Imperial International Exhibition of 1909. It housed a large plaster-cast statue of King Edward VII, unveiled a few days after the opening ceremony on 20 May. The Exhibition had displays from a number of countries, including Austria, China, Denmark, Holland, Italy, Persia and Russia.

A scene from the Coronation Exhibition of 1911 at the White City, in the year of George V's crowning. Exhibits included models of the Taj Mahal, the Palace of Delhi, the Pagan Temple of Burma and the Golden Monastery of Mandalay. The photograph shows how some interiors at the White City were made of a mixture of scaled down replica buildings, painted backdrops and draperies that hid the ceilings.

The Flip-Flap at the White City was a giant machine with two arms 150ft-long, each with a passenger car at the end. When in motion the trip took three minutes as each arm rotated 180 degrees, passing the other at the top. The photograph shows the Flip-Flap being demolished in 1937 by workmen from the local firm of George Cohen Sons and Company Ltd.

Industries

Until the mid-19th century both Hammersmith and Fulham were predominantly rural, the main employment opportunities being agriculture and market gardening, riverside work for boat builders, fishermen and watermen, and stables, inns and forges on the western roads leading out of London. Away from the river a number of industries had become established by the beginning of the 19th century, notably breweries and malthouses, brickmaking and wax manufacture in Hammersmith, and the pottery founded in Fulham by John Dwight in 1671.

Two factors seem to have been responsible for the growth of industry. Firstly, the proximity of the area to London and to the transport possibilities offered by the river, and secondly, the availability of a local workforce when the population grew. From the 1850s onwards there was much house building, which provided work and increased the population. The population of the borough grew rapidly, from 10,028 in 1801 to 249,482 in 1901, including labourers who arrived from Ireland from the 1840s to work in the market gardens and building sites. One of the earliest modern industrial enterprises in the borough was Fulham Gas Works, founded in 1824 by the Imperial Gas Company on the Sandford Manor House site by Chelsea Creek. As late as the 1970s some 2,000 people were employed in the gas works and in the various adjacent Gas Board offices, but these have all since closed.

The wharves that developed along the river and around the bridges became important locations for the loading and unloading of goods such as timber, corn, coal and building materials, and heavy industry was also sited behind the wharves. In Hammersmith, lead mills, malt houses and boat builders clustered around the Creek, which was the outflow of the Stamford Brook until it was filled in 1936 and the Brook culverted. Other industrial concerns in Hammersmith and below the bridge included the Albert Oil Mills in Upper Mall, Vosper's boat building business at the Creek, Clarke's Phoenix Lead Mills in Lower Mall, Gwynne's Iron Works in Crisp Road and Rosser and Russell's heating, ventilation and hydraulic engineering works at Queens Wharf. The building firm of George Wimpey and Co. started in Hammersmith Grove in 1880. In Fulham the Anglo-American Oil Company had established a wharf at Crabtree, later the Esso depot, by the turn of the last century. A number of oil companies eventually had premises in Fulham, including the Shell-Mex BP depot and Total in Townmead Road, Petrofina in Carnwath Road and Duckham and Co. in Rainville Road.

Many other manufacturing or processing businesses in the borough were small, occupying cramped sites in residential areas. Two noxious trades are listed in the mid 19th century Fulham censuses: bone cutters and fat melters (working in the Bone Sheds), and the Sewer Manure Company. In the late 19th century the underground railway came to the area, providing not only the opportunity to commute to employment further away but also jobs nearer home. In 1899 Charles Booth listed the main local industries in Fulham as railway and omnibus works, the building trade, the gas works, market gardening and laundries. Many women worked in the laundries.

A significant portion of the borough's industries have been in the food and drink sector. There were a number of breweries, such as Stansfeld's (formerly the Swan Brewery, Walham Green), which closed in 1928, Kop's Brewery in Townmead Road, makers of non-alcoholic Kop's Ale, and the Hammersmith Distillery. The big sugar works of Manbré and Garton first came to Brandenburgh House estate south of Hammersmith Bridge in 1873, manufacturing sugar for the brewing industry as well as saccharine, glucose, syrup and treacle. The factory was demolished in 1979. J. Lyons and Co. had bakeries, an ice-cream factory and offices on their extensive main site at Cadby Hall in Hammersmith Road, which was redeveloped in the 1980s. Fuller's made cakes and chocolates in Great Church Lane (now Talgarth Road) between 1900 and 1964, while Macfarlane, Lang and Company had a large biscuit factory in Town-mead Road between 1903 and the 1930s.

Local electricity businesses included the Osram Works at Brook Green, Julius Sax, who made electrical components, and Edgar's, gas engineers at the Blenheim Works, Lower Mall. Fulham Power Station was a municipal enterprise, built in 1901 and served by a fleet of colliers owned and operated by Fulham Metropolitan Borough Council before World War Two, all with the name *Fulham*. The power station closed in 1978 and the site has been redeveloped. Until 1966 there was also a small power station in Hammersmith, just below Hammersmith Bridge.

In the 1960s there were still some 400 factories in Hammersmith, especially in the north of the area, including a Rolls-Royce works in Hythe Road, but many have now closed. Further south the riverside industries in Hammersmith were brought to an end by both wartime bombing and the redevelopment of the riverside area. In Fulham, the unsuitability of the roads for large-scale road haulage has meant that the majority of big firms have moved away and their sites are now being developed for residential or mixed use. Today the main employers in the borough are the BBC, the local authority, service industries and offices. The Borough Profile of 1998 notes that during the 1990s the decline in the manufacturing sector continued, partly compensated by an expansion of jobs in the service industry. Data from the 1991 census indicates that 85% of residents worked in service industries, while only 11% worked in manufacturing and construction industries and the number of the latter fell by a third during the 1980s. In the mid 1990s 23% of floor space in the borough in employment-generating uses was office space, only 5% industrial. These figures confirm that there has been a decisive shift in the borough since World War Two away from industry in favour of offices, while on the river the land vacated by the disappearing factories has been redeveloped for mixed residential and commercial uses.

Ruel's crucible factory in the 19th century. The enterprise, started by a Mr Ruel from Germany, was located first at Chelsea, then at Fulham and finally in Shepherds Bush. The crucibles ranged in size from egg-cup to two gallon jars, and were supplied to the Royal Mint, chemists and gold refiners. Other early industrial activity in Hammersmith included brickmaking, bleachfields and a wax manufactory near Ravenscourt Park.

A scene at Fulham Gas Works in about 1880. The gas works was founded when the Sandford Manor site in Imperial Road was acquired by The Imperial Gas Company in 1824, and the first gas holder, now listed, was built in 1830. Eventually the works employed some 2,500 people, but it was closed in the 1970s. The photograph shows the gas purification tanks adjacent to Gasholder no.4.

This photograph of Fulham Power Station was taken in 1968. The power station was built in 1936 by Fulham Borough Council on the site of an earlier facility dating from the turn of the century. After the war it became the largest municipal power station in the country. It was nationalised in 1948, but eventually became obsolete and was demolished in 1983. The exclusive Harbour Club now occupies the site.

Employees at J. O'Connor, motor haulage contractors of 40-42 Disbrowe Road, Fulham, photographed in the 1920s. The transition from the use of horses to motor vehicles for haulage was not yet complete. Kelly's local directories list the firm of O'Connor as greengrocers and later firewood dealers from 1906–7 until 1920-1, when they appear for the first time as haulage contractors. The business remained in Disbrowe Road until the early 1960s.

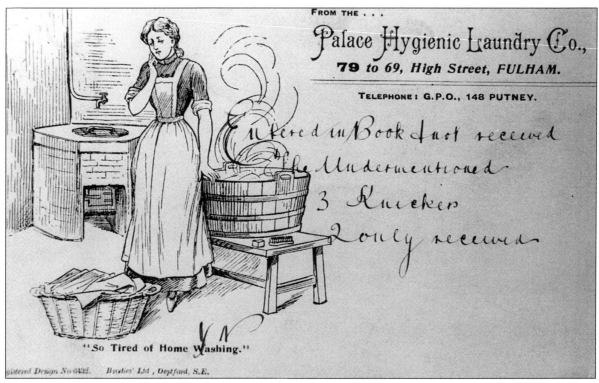

An amusing and graphic heading for the bills and receipts of the Palace Hygienic Laundry Company, 69-79 High Street, Fulham, in existence in the early 20th century. The Palace was one of several laundries in Fulham, including the Sunlight Laundry, Claxton Laundry, Carnwath Laundry, Whitewash Laundry and Madame A. Noel's French Laundry.

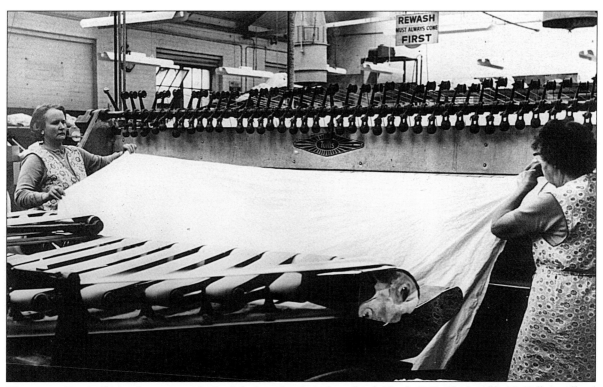

Women working in the ironing room at the Sunlight Laundry, Broughton Road, March 1939. The laundries in Fulham offered a valuable source of employment for local women. The Sunlight Laundry was started in about 1900 and had over 12,000 square feet of premises. The laundry's old building now houses a community centre and Sands End Library.

Employees of Waring and Gillow making field tents in the former Machinery Hall at the White City during World War One. The large shed-like structures of the White City exhibition site proved ideal for wartime purposes. At first Belgian refugees were accommodated there, and later up to 8,000 workers manufactured aeroplane parts, tents, gas masks and other military equipment.

Waring and Gillow also made De Havilland aeroplane bodies at their Alliance Aeroplane factory in Cambridge Road (now Cambridge Grove), 1914–18. The firm of S.J. Waring and Sons first appears there in the rate books in 1899. Between the wars the company manufactured furniture and provided panelling and interior fittings for many stately homes and Cunard liners. Waring and Gillow remained in Cambridge Grove until the mid-1950s.

Salesmen from the Bluebell Polish Company and their handcart, c.1900. The office and works of the company were near the river at Townmead Road, then at Carnwath Road and later De Morgan Road, and they also had premises in Manchester. They were taken over by Reckitt and Colman and the works continued to be listed at De Morgan Road in the Kelly's Post Office London Directories *until 1959.*

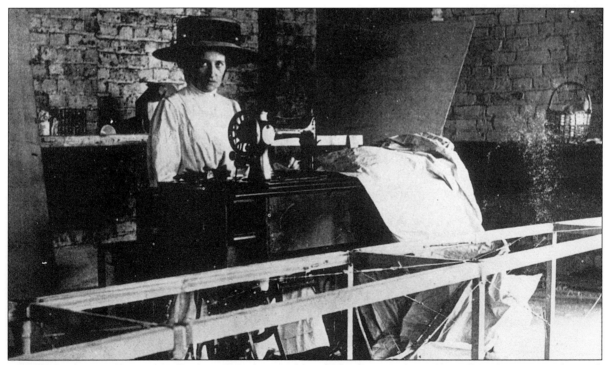

Louie, wife of Sir Geoffrey De Havilland, stitching the wing fabric for his first aeroplane. Sir Geoffrey, the aviator and aircraft designer, built his first two aeroplanes in a loft over a factory in Bothwell Street, Fulham, in 1909–10. The engines were made by a car company in Willesden. His first flight ended in disaster, as the plane crashed on take-off, but trials of the second were more successful.

Mr Albert Young making brushes at 160 Railway Approach, Shepherds Bush, in the 1920s. The photograph illustrates one of the many small businesses that used to be in the borough, located in cramped premises and employing one or two people in various crafts and trades. Other businesses in Railway Approach at that time included a watchmaker, a woodturner and two umbrella makers, as well as shops and antiques dealers.

Repairing pipes at the Imperial Tobacco Company Ltd, 1907. The firm, which was later known as the Civic Company Ltd, had premises at 79-83 Fulham Palace Road. It produced mainly pipes and other smokers' goods. The company is listed in commercial directories until the late 1960s.

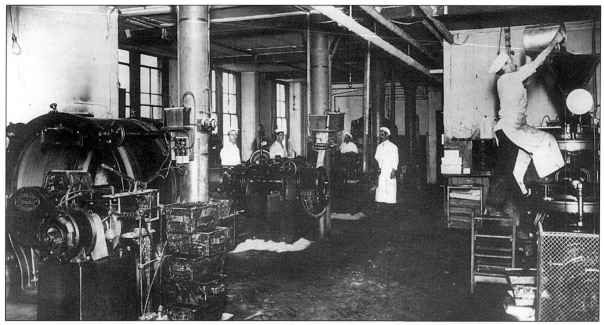

Making chocolate in 1909 at Fuller's, who had a factory in Great Church Lane (now Talgarth Road), where they also made their famous walnut cakes. William Bruce Fuller, an American, founded the company in 1889 in central London, and the factory relocated to Hammersmith in 1900. The site, where some 1,000 people eventually worked, was sold to the Council in 1964, and a year later Fuller's moved to Birmingham.

This illustration of Messrs Cadby's Pianoforte Manufactory appeared in The Builder *in 1874. The company had been set up by Charles Cadby in 1839, and moved to this handsome new building in Hammersmith Road from its previous premises in Clerkenwell. The keystones of the windows on the front façade contained carved portraits of eminent composers. The company was operating in a very competitive market, and it closed in the 1880s.*

The mixing room in the bread bakery at Cadby Hall, J. Lyons and Company's extensive premises in Hammersmith Road. This 1951 photograph shows the dough being mixed in vats before being placed in tins for baking. In 1894 Lyons bought part of the Cadby Hall site, formerly occupied by Charles Cadby's piano factory, and the company later expanded to become a major local employer until Cadby Hall's demolition in 1983.

A view of Manbré and Garton's sugar factory in 1977, two years before it was demolished. The firm of Manbré, which moved in 1876 from Spitalfields to the Brandenburgh House estate site south of Hammersmith Bridge, merged in 1926 with a Battersea company founded by William Garton in 1855. Both companies started with the same aim of making a new brewing sugar to enable lighter beer to be produced.

Sugar is unloaded from a barge at Manbré and Garton. The company developed into a multi-national concern for the refining of cane sugars, processing of maize and manufacture of sugar and starch products. Eventually the narrow surrounding streets were unable to cope with the tankers that took away the products. Some of the factory areas had attractive names, such as the sugar candy houses and the syrup room.

Children of the employees of Joseph Edward Beckett, lighterman and wharfinger of Dorset Wharf in Rainville Road, Fulham, enjoy an outing in 1926. A lighterman is involved in loading and unloading goods from a lighter, or flat-bottomed barge, and a wharfinger owns or manages wharves. Unfortunately, the gentleman standing third from left was drowned three years later, a reminder of the dangers of the river.

Staff and guests at the Vitamins factory, Upper Mall, watching the Boat Race in 1949. The Vitamins factory was founded in 1927 and came to Hammersmith in 1930, together with a sister company named Agricultural Food Products Ltd. They chiefly made a wheatgerm product called Bemax. By the 1950s some of the production had been moved to Crawley, and the company finally left Hammersmith in the mid-1970s.

From 1937 onwards both the Oxford and Cambridge boats for the Boat Race were usually built at the boathouse of G. Sims at 15 Lower Mall, by the Rutland public house. The business was there from 1936 to 1955. This photograph shows the Oxford boat under construction for the race that took place on 29 March 1947, when Cambridge won by 10 lengths.

Gwynne's stood on the site of the Riverside Studios in Hammersmith. The company was founded in 1849 in the Strand for the manufacture of centrifugal pumps, and in 1903 merged with Hammersmith Iron Works at Chancellors Wharf. Later Gwynne's made aero engines and (in Chiswick) cars. They went into liquidation in 1925, and in 1927 a successor company was moved to Lincoln, although an office remained in Hammersmith until about 1966.

Hammersmith Distillery was started in 1857 on the site of Brandenburgh House, and acquired by the Distillers Company in 1919. Industrial chemicals became the main product, and molasses was brought up by barge from an associated distillery in Dagenham and stored in huge tanks on the site, while lorries took away the products of industrial alcohol, methylated spirits and carbon dioxide. After 1959 the site was devoted to research only.

Two views of Blake's Wharf, Stevenage Road, in about 1932. Munitions were made on the site during World War One, and Blake's were established there in 1920. By the date of the photograph the wharves covered 3.5 acres. The firm was engaged in the warehousing, storage and packing business, and dealt with a variety of goods that included paper, foodstuffs, cars, aeroplanes and machinery. Before the war barges left the wharves daily to take goods to the steamship lines for onward transportation worldwide. The wharves were demolished in the 1970s.

Filling barrels at the Shell-Mex BP Ltd oil terminal at Lensbury Wharf in Townmead Road, sometime before World War Two. In 1910 BP applied to the London County Council to store 200,000 gallons of petrol at the site, to be conveyed up and down the river on licensed barges. BP remained there until the late 1980s. They were one of a number of oil companies with premises on the Fulham riverfront.

The 1920-1 Osram Tower at the Osram Works at Brook Green, 1975. Robertson Electric Lamps Ltd opened on the site in 1893, and the complex evolution of the company, which was eventually owned by GEC included the formation of a subsidiary company called MO Valves to manufacture valves. The factory closed in 1988 and, apart from the tower, the buildings were replaced by a Tesco supermarket and housing.

Index